BEHIND
CLOSED DOORS

PAMELA J. NEWMAN, PH.D.

Managing Director
Marsh & McLennan, Incorporated

ALFRED F. LYNCH

Manager of Corporate Planning
JC Penney Company, Inc.

BEHIND CLOSED DOORS:
A GUIDE
TO SUCCESSFUL
MEETINGS

PRENTICE-HALL, INC., *Englewood Cliffs, New Jersey* 07632

Library of Congress Cataloging in Publication Data

NEWMAN, PAMELA JANE.
   Behind closed doors.

   Bibliography: p.
   1. Corporate meetings. I. Lynch, Alfred F.
II. Title.
HD2743.N525 1983   658.4'563   82-20509
ISBN 0-13-072025-9

Editorial/production supervision
and interior design: Virginia Huebner
Cover design: Jeannette Jacobs
Manufacturing buyer: Anthony Caruso
Page makeup: Patricia Deniz

©1983 by Prentice-Hall, Inc., Englewood Cliffs, New Jersey 07632

Printed in the United States of America

10 9 8 7 6 5 4 3 2 1

ISBN 0-13-072025-9

PRENTICE-HALL INTERNATIONAL, INC., *London*
PRENTICE-HALL OF AUSTRALIA PTY. LIMITED, *Sydney*
EDITORA PRENTICE-HALL DO BRASIL, Ltda., *Rio de Janeiro*
PRENTICE-HALL CANADA INC., *Toronto*
PRENTICE-HALL OF INDIA PRIVATE LIMITED, *New Delhi*
PRENTICE-HALL OF JAPAN, INC., *Tokyo*
PRENTICE-HALL OF SOUTHEAST ASIA PTE. LTD., *Singapore*
WHITEHALL BOOKS LIMITED, *Wellington, New Zealand*

We would like to dedicate this book to our families: William, Romy, and Theodore; Patricia, Sharon, Jeffrey, David, Cathleen, and Stephen.

CONTENTS

CHECKLISTS

FORMS

EXAMPLES

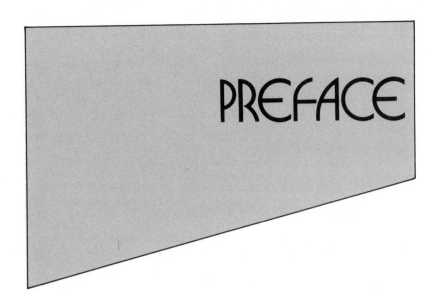

PREFACE

Our purpose in writing this book was to provide a guide for organizing and conducting business meetings. We believe that the basics of all meetings are the same regardless of size—from one-on-one to one hundred. Our examples, however, are for groups of from six to eight. The specific process you use during your meetings will vary; however, the why's and how to's of planning a meeting are basic.

As you read this book, keep in mind that we feel the how to's presented apply to situations that most managers don't think of as "meetings," but perform during their normal day-to-day activities: one-on-one interchanges with their boss or a review with a subordinate. We believe that most managers should think of these situations as true meetings and thus prepare for them as they would for any group meeting. Consequently, we've included a chapter entitled, "One-On-One Meetings" for those meetings with your manager or subordinate.

Our aim is to allow the reader to recognize the complicated dynamics involved when people come together and to share tools that will have a positive influence on the dynamics. Our objective is thus to give you a meeting management tool that will enable you to get results. You will learn how to prepare for a meeting, how to plan an agenda, how to conduct a meeting, and how to evaluate its success.

At the end of each chapter, we have included checklists. These can be used as a handy reference tool or we suggest that you reproduce whatever form is appropriate and make enough copies so that you and your coworkers can use one for each meeting you run or attend. You will also have it available to support your associates' efforts when they plan or lead meetings.

We sincerely hope that this guide will improve the effectiveness and efficiency of your next meeting.

ACKNOWLEDGEMENTS

It is not possible to acknowledge all those friends and business acquaintances who have shared their frustrations with running and attending meetings, but we must record our debt to Norah Edelmann for assistance and editing of the original manuscript. We must also recognize the professional administrative support of Eileen Ribowsky.

Finally, we would both like to thank our families for their patience under many trials and a few "closed doors." Without their support, this work could not have been completed.

New York, New York   PAMELA J. NEWMAN

                                         ALFRED F. LYNCH

BEHIND CLOSED DOORS

INTRODUCTION

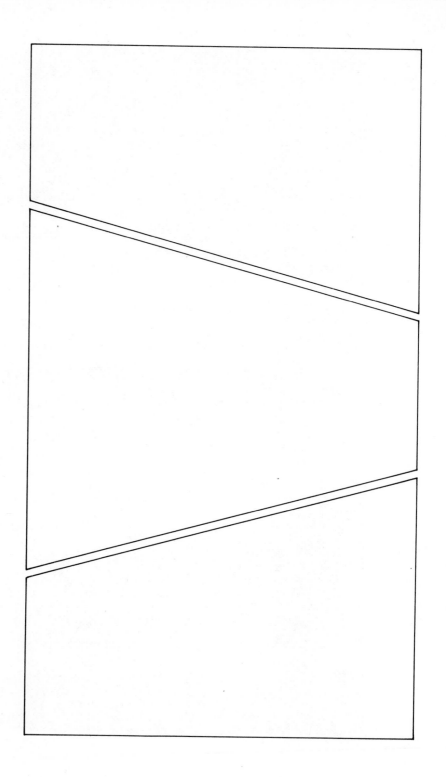

I was in my car and on the road half an hour ahead of my usual schedule so that I would be at an 8:30 meeting on time. Well, it didn't turn out that way. Due to a minor rear-end collision a mile and a half up the road, I sat for nearly an hour and a half waiting for the traffic to move. According to radio reports, there was difficulty getting the tow trucks through the unusually heavy morning-rush-hour traffic to the scene of the accident.

The meeting was held at 8:30. I arrived at 10:45. Needless to add, I missed the meeting. But as it turned out, it didn't matter. In a five-minute phone conversation with my manager, I found out all I needed to know. The meeting lasted two hours. I had to admit I was secretly glad I'd been stuck in that traffic jam; I was able to work on some reports while I waited.

The fact is, according to Anthony Jay, Chairman of Video Arts Ltd., a London-based producer of training films for business, in the United States as many as 100,000 meetings are held each month. If a minimum of thirty minutes is required for each meeting and if each meeting is attended by an average of four individuals, almost 2½ million hours are spent in meetings each year. Think of the hourly rate for most people involved in your meetings. Multiply this hourly rate by 2½ million. As you can see, the dollar cost of meetings in the United States is staggering.

In an evaluation of the effectiveness of their meetings, a pharmaceutical firm in New York City determined that they could save time by eliminating their weekly sales review meeting. Their study showed that a memorandum concerning sales results was even more effective. The result was that since on the average at least four people attended each meeting, forty hours or one full workweek a month was saved by issuing a memorandum and not having the weekly sales review meeting.

Efficient use of meeting time has a purpose, we believe. Both Dr. Newman, Managing Director of Marsh and McLennan, Incorporated, who develops and designs programs utilizing group dynamics, organizational behavior, and networking techniques for results-oriented management meetings, and I, a former data processing consultant, manager of training and development programs, and now Manager of Corporate Planning are frequently called upon to design, conduct, and evaluate meetings.

Both of us agreed when we met to discuss meeting dynamics that the most frequent comments we hear after most meetings ran in this vein: "What a total waste of time!" "We didn't accomplish anything." "I don't know why I was invited; I really didn't have to be there." "The meeting was too long." "One person dominated the entire meeting." "The agenda listed four topics and we only covered one."

These and similar comments were the subject of our conversations at several business meetings. At one point we decided to combine our observations and write down our own insights as to how meeting malaise could be eliminated. This book is the result of those efforts.

KNOW
YOUR PURPOSE

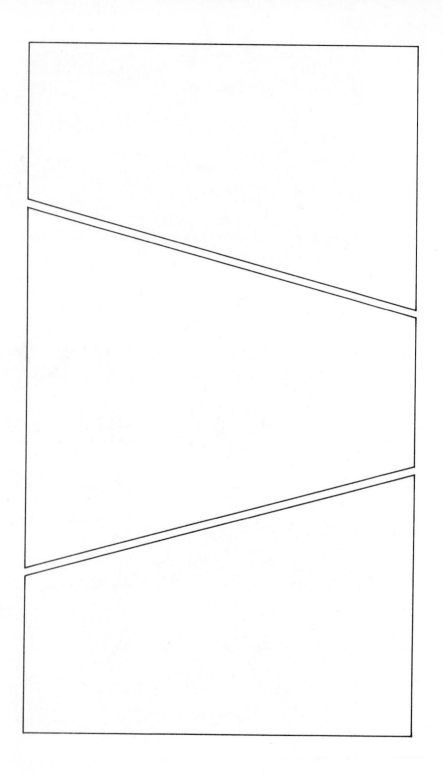

In preparing to write this book, one of the questions we asked was: "Why does management hold meetings, and what usually occurs during these meetings?"

From our research we learned that there are six basic reasons to hold meetings:

1. Information presentation and exchange

2. Project collaboration, coordination, and communication

3. Conflict resolution/crisis coping

4. Trend analysis and future planning

5. Improvement of existing work

6. Training and development

Briefly, here is what generally occurs at these meetings.

1.   INFORMATION PRESENTATION AND EXCHANGE

This is the most common reason for holding a meeting. The purpose is to share information and to answer questions.

2.   PROJECT COLLABORATION, COORDINATION, AND COMMUNICATION

This type of meeting is held to establish work objectives. However, in many instances, people may be reluctant to attend such a meeting, preferring to do work at hand to planning future work. To be effective, everyone involved in a project should attend such meetings. It will be helpful to give a typical example of just how effective project collaboration meetings can be.

A complex data processing project called for delivery of a system to support the introduction of a new computer software system. During this project a meeting was held once a week to accomplish two objectives:

1.   To keep all project personnel informed as to the status of the project

2.   To answer questions concerning problems being experienced by project personnel

The average length of each meeting was approximately an hour and a half. A critical objective was that the work be completed on time. Each team member came to the meeting with the current status of his or her assignment, what they hoped to accomplish before the next meeting, and a review by team members of any client-related problems.

Due to marketing pressures, about halfway through the project, the client asked if the system could be completed six weeks earlier than the contract stipulated. As an incentive, the client offered a $50,000 bonus to be paid if this more exacting schedule could be met. As a result of the regular team effort of the weekly project meetings, the team was able to promise and deliver a completed project seven weeks ahead of schedule.

The purpose of these project collaboration, coordination, and communication meetings was results-oriented. They kept everyone informed of the status of the work assigned and proved invaluable in meeting the tighter schedule.

Another variation of the project collaboration meeting is a fact-finding meeting. This is usually held when a crisis occurs. For example, if the purpose is to determine all the facts in a particular situation, the participants are generally told this before the meeting. At the meeting, the participants are given a chance to air their points of view and share their fund of knowledge. Any judgments or conclusions are suspended for a later time.

3. CONFLICT RESOLUTION/CRISIS COPING

One of the most difficult types of meetings to hold are those designed to resolve conflict. This is because meeting participants tend to get emotional. Everyone, including the meeting leader, should try to remain calm and cool. This is easier to accomplish if, before the meeting is held, the meeting leader asks these questions:

1. Who is involved in the crisis or conflict?

2. Have these people been invited to attend?

3. Should I research the problem?

4. Do I have all the information I need to resolve this conflict?

5. If not, where can I get it?

6. How much time should the meeting take?

Remember Lynch's Law:

THE MORE TIME SPENT GATHERING THE FACTS BEFORE THE MEETING, THE SHORTER THE MEETING.

The meeting leader benefits when the meeting agenda is held firm. For example, if you set the meeting time for an hour and there are four people in attendance, each person gets a fixed and preannounced amount of time to present his or her views. Ten minutes is reserved for a contingency discussion period. This format keeps a conflict moving toward resolution rather than exacerbating the tension.

Distributing in advance a statement of purpose for this type of meeting clarifies the aim. An example:

> Each one of you will have an opportunity to describe your understanding of our conflict, the alternatives you have considered, and the one you recommend. You may wish to allow three minutes to present your analysis of the problem, four minutes for your alternatives, and three minutes for your recommendations.

In summary, time restrictions often diffuse the anger and tension inherent in a conflict-resolution meeting.

4.   TREND ANALYSIS AND STRATEGIC PLANNING

If the purpose of the meeting is to, let's say, review or analyze sales trends, or to plan for future growth, four qualities must be present for success:

1.   A well-prepared agenda will have been written to guide the thought process.

2. A systematic methodology will be employed to develop the views of all present.

3. Innovative thinking will be encouraged. The fragile quality of a new idea will be respected.

4. Specific outcomes will be sought so that satisfaction is felt by all.

5. IMPROVEMENT OF EXISTING WORK

A meeting may be held to discuss the improvement of ongoing work. Unfortunately, these meetings are often failures because of a meeting managment style depicted in the following cartoon:

". . . all those against, signify by tendering their resignations."

(Courtesy of Nick Hobart, "Pepper . . . and Salt," *The Wall Street Journal.*)

Unlike our cartoon example, successfully run meetings of this type allow participants to "Tell it like it is."

6. TRAINING AND DEVELOPMENT

Training employees is an essential part of any manager's job. The meeting leader needs to know who the audience is, their expectations, fears, and motivations, and then be able to determine the best approach to meeting the training needs of the group.

To conduct this type of meeting, the leader determines the skill level of the people to be trained, the materials required for the training, and clarifies the desired change in behavior as a result of the training.

The training meeting environment must meet these criteria:

1. The learning is active rather than passive.

2. Learning is enhanced through association rather than rote memory.

3. The environment is positive and supportive.

4. The leader has a measurement device that measures the trainees' level of learning.

These points are elaborated on below.

1.   *The Learning Is Active Rather than Passive.*

People retain knowledge more easily when they are actively involved in acquiring knowledge. The driver school failure rate is less than one-half of 1%—a phenomenon directly correlated to the involvement the student has in learning the technique of driving.

2.   *Learning Is Enhanced Through Association Rather than Rote Memory.*

People find it easier to retain information when it is associated with something they already know. This is why it is easier to remember someone's name when you associate it with a concept with which you are already familiar rather than relying on simple memorization of the new name.

3.   *The Training Environment Must Be Positive and Supportive.*

Fear, anger, and resentment are all learning "demotivations." They block out a trainee's ability to concentrate on what is to be learned. We once met a trainee in the Lamaze system of childbirth who became so frightened by the knowledge that she would be required to have an intravenous device hooked to her arm during labor that she never heard a word of the instructions regarding what she was to do during labor. Had the meeting leader been more sensitive, she might have recognized the trainee's fear, discussed it, and been able to reduce it so that continued learning could take place.

4.   *The Leader Has a Measurement Device that Measures the Trainees' Level of Learning.*

Too often people leave a learning environment having understood little of what they were being taught—and the leader never knows it. Great teachers know that the burden of proof is on them to make sure that the participant really understands. Watch any parent toilet train a child to see this principle in action.

SUMMARY

As you know from your own experience, there are many other reasons meetings might be held that we could have included here. However, these six functions serve as a foundation for the meetings management holds in most businesses each day in companies throughout the world.

Using the "Meeting Types Checklist" that follows, estimate the number of times during the past three months that you have held or attended each of the six types of meetings listed. This will help you pinpoint the most common meeting type you are holding or attending.

Once you've listed the types of meetings you have held or attended in the past three months, we recommend that you record the date of the next meeting and the name of the person who will lead it. The remainder of this book will help you make sure that the meeting meets its stated objective, produces results, and allows participants to leave the meeting room invigorated and committed.

MEETING TYPES CHECKLIST

MEETING/TYPE	NUMBER HELD IN LAST THREE MONTHS	DATE OF NEXT MEETING	ASSIGNED MEETING LEADER
1. Information Presentation and Exchange			
2. Project Collaboration, Coordination, and Communication			
3. Conflict Resolution/ Crisis Coping			
4. Trend Analysis and Future Planning			
5. Improvements of Existing Work			
6. Training and Development			
Others:			
a.			
b.			
c.			
d.			
e.			

KNOW
YOUR OBJECTIVE

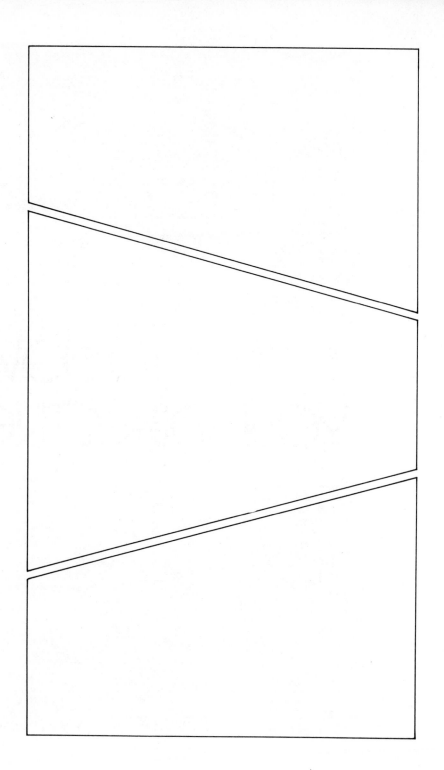

Every meeting should begin with one all-important first question. This question is the very foundation for every successful meeting:

IS THIS MEETING NECESSARY?

Once you have asked this question, answer it by

STATING THE OBJECTIVE OF THE MEETING IN ONE SENTENCE

This statement of aim must be

- Results-oriented
- Measurable
- "Do-able"

Here are two examples. The first is an ineffective statement of objective:

"We will meet to discuss the new retirement plan."

The second statement is an effective statement of objective:

"The purpose of the meeting is to explain three sections of the company's new retirement policy in a one-hour meeting."

Once you have a clear statement of objective for your meeting, ask:

"Instead of having a face-to-face meeting, can I handle this matter by phone?"

or

"Will a memo do the job?"

Here's an example. Let's say the objective of your meeting is to introduce a new policy. A before-the-meeting review of the policy could be more meaningful, provided that a memo is sent stating the policy clearly and announcing that a meeting will be held the following week to answer questions concerning the policy.

A memo allows the people who will attend the meeting an opportunity to organize their questions. They're involved. And because they're involved, not only will your meeting be more interesting, it will also accomplish your aim to answer any questions that might arise about the new policy.

Knowing the objective of your meeting will also enable you to know your desired outcome. For example, a meeting may result in:

1. A follow-up meeting to explore the issues further

2. A series of regular meetings held to monitor the progress of ongoing activities

3. A resolution to be passed which effects a change

4. A finished product or plan

MEETING ALTERNATIVES

The aim you seek will best be accomplished by holding a face-to-face meeting if none of the alternatives described below are acceptable.

MEETING ALTERNATIVES CHECKLIST

ALTERNATIVE ACTION	YES	NO
● Does the objective require consultation?		
● Can consultation be handled by phone or conference call as well as in person?		
● Should I postpone the meeting to develop more preliminary data?		
● Can the meeting be canceled to no one's disadvantage?		

If you answer "yes" to any of the four alternative actions, you may have saved everyone time and prevented an unnecessary meeting.

PLANNING

If you have completed your alternative checklist and a meeting is still called for, the next question becomes: How do you plan for the meeting?

The first idea is to think of the plan as two separate, yet related questions:

- Desired results or outcomes
- Who will or should attend

In this chapter we explore the desired results or outcomes and resources. Who should attend is discussed in the following chapter.

Let's go back to the example offered earlier to describe an effective statement of purpose.

Our example was: "The purpose of the meeting is to explain three sections of the company's new retirement policy in a one-hour meeting." To plan for the achievement of this purpose, the meeting leader had to do some in-depth meeting planning. The planning required identifying (1) desired outcome and/or expected results, (2) resources or experiences required to achieve those results, and (3) of all the desired outcomes, which was most imperative.

All the desired outcomes or expected results for explaining the retirement policy were brainstormed and recorded by the meeting leader. Once all the outcomes were identified and the most important outcome was selected, the resources necessary to make the meeting effective were also brainstormed.

The meeting leader's planning sheet is shown on **page** 23.

The key to success was the question:

"If only one of these can be covered, which outcome is the most important?"

In this example, "point out three key changes" was the central concept. Restricting the meeting to this idea produced the effective statement of purpose:

"The purpose of the meeting is to review three sections of the company's new retirement policy in a one-hour meeting."

Identifying the purpose was the result of brainstorming all the possible outcomes and identifying the one with the highest priority. This resulted in a single-focus item that could be handled in an hour. At this point, the resources needed to support the single focus of the meeting were identified and prioritized.

We recommend that you generate your desired outcomes first. Once they are clear to you, generate a list of resources needed to support these outcomes. Practice will make this work for you. The following planning hints will also improve your meetings.

MEETING: 12/2/82 TO EXPLAIN NEW RETIREMENT POLICY

DESIRED OUTCOMES OR EXPECTED RESULTS	RESOURCES REQUIRED
• Discuss new retirement plan	• Copies of plan
• Review benefits of plan	• List of benefits
• Compare old with new	• Chart showing old and new
• Point out three key changes— *most imperative	• Describe three key changes
• Answer any questions	• Generate list of possible questions

HINTS ON PLANNING

1. "Running by the seat of your pants" may take less advance time than planning a meeting. Remember, however, that time is money, and the participants want a productive experience. Careful planning will reduce the likelihood of meetings being held that fail to accomplish their aim. Remember Newman's Law:

IF YOU CAN'T PLAN IT—YOU CAN'T DO IT.

2. Planning will help you determine if you're trying to cover too much too fast.

3. Planning the resources and experiences necessary to achieve the aim will help ensure that you have at your fingertips the material that will allow you to achieve your aim.

4. When planning you may want to use a flipchart (particularly when planning with others) or you can work on your own with a plain sheet of paper. In either case, we suggest that you make three columns (see the "Meeting Planning Form" on page 25):

   a. Column 1: Desired Outcomes or Expected Results. Once you've identified all the desired outcomes or expected results, be sure that you select the ones you can accomplish in the time you have for the meeting.

   b. Column 2: Who Should Attend. Determine all the resources you have available to you which will help you achieve your aim.

   c. Column 3: Resources Required. Then consider everyone who could attend the meeting. Ask the question: Is there anything in the background, value system, experience, or reporting relationships of the possible attendees that will assist me in achieving or prevent me from achieving my desired outcome or expected results? This part of the planning will help make your meeting more effective since you can prepare for expected roadblocks or call on those in attendance to help you achieve your expectation.

(The next chapter will help you do a better job with this part of the planning process.)

MEETING PLANNING FORM

(1)	(2)	(3)
DESIRED OUTCOMES OR EXPECTED RESULTS	WHO SHOULD ATTEND	RESOURCES REQUIRED

After you think you have determined the desired outcome and resources needed, stop the brainstorming process by completing the following "Meeting Purpose Checklist."

MEETING PURPOSE CHECKLIST

ACTIVITY	YES	NO
• Did I state the purpose in a single sentence?		
• Did I consider other alternatives?		
• Did I identify the expected outcomes?		
• Did I make sure that the expected outcomes were realistic?		
• Did I identify the resources required?		
• Did I identify the most important outcome?		

KNOW
YOUR AUDIENCE

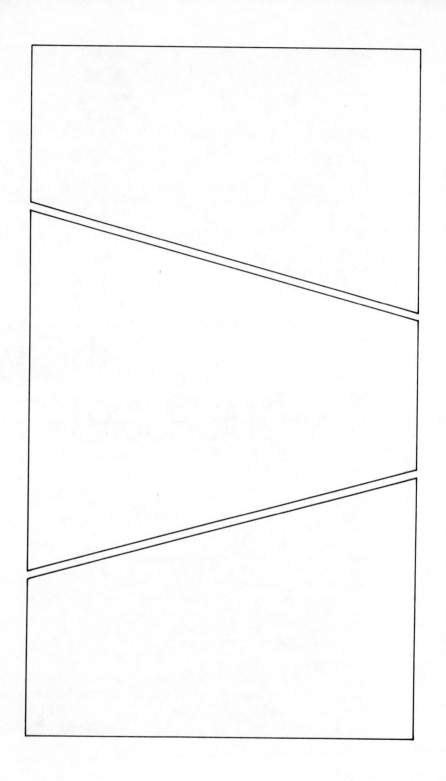

Thim chapter reviews techniques
that meeting leaders should use to learn:

1. How to understand who is in the audience

2. How to remember the name of each person at a meeting

3. How to address people at meetings

4. How to plan a strategy for a presentation that will help persuade an audience

In 1971, Al Capp, the cartoonist, was the most highly paid college campus speaker in the United States. He earned $6,000 for each college campus presentation he made. However, as he spoke to a packed house at Hill Auditorium at the University of Michigan about the need for conservation in America, loud cat calls, hoots, and jeers forced him to leave the stage 15

minutes into his presentation. He left for the airport immediately. What happened to Al Capp? Capp failed to do his
homework. He didn't *know his audience*, so the comments he
made alienated them.

Less dramatic but equally serious incidents occur almost daily in
business meetings. However, the meeting leader who knows who
the meeting participants are will avoid meeting conflict, tension,
and possible total disruption.

Knowing your participants—the size of the group, organizational level, skill level, expectations, and interest level—will help
you design the meeting and help you avoid the mistake that Al
Capp made at the University of Michigan.

In the chapter "Know Your Purpose," the related events of
"desired results or outcomes" and "resources or experiences"
were described for a retirement plan meeting. The next step is to
determine who will attend. A suggested list is provided below.

Here's a summary of the brainstorming effort:

DESIRED OUTCOMES OR EXPECTED RESULTS	WHO WILL ATTEND?	RESOURCES OR EXPERIENCES REQUIRED
• Discuss new retirement plan	• Six new employees: six months to a year of experience; just starting careers	• Copies of plan
• Review benefits of plan		• List of benefits
• Compare old with new		• Chart showing old and new
• State purpose of changes	• Six retiring employees: retiring in a year; want to know effect on their plans	• Generate list of all changes
• Answer any questions		• Generate list of possible questions

The results of the audience analysis indicates that two meetings are probably necessary: one with the six new employees and one with the six employees about to retire. Why? Their needs and expectations are so different that a single meeting would not meet the divergent needs.

HOW CAN I IDENTIFY THE NEEDS OF THE PARTICIPANTS?

As was evident from our example, the concerns and the needs of the participants must be dealt with if a meeting is going to be successful. To determine what these needs are ahead of time, you may have to send out a questionnaire, conduct a telephone interview to gather a sample, or try any other way of eliciting from participants their needs, interests, priorities, and expectations. If none of this can be done beforehand, a census of needs and expectations can be taken at the beginning of the meeting itself.

Determining the needs of a group within your company may be easier than doing the same with a group outside your company. Here's an example of what can happen when you don't meet the needs of an outside group:

A management consultant met with a group of real estate executives whom she had never met. She presented a very theoretical model of how they could better manage their business. Gradually, each of the executives developed blank, bored looks as they listened to her comments.

Once the unsuccessful meeting was over, she analyzed what went wrong. The consultant realized how little she had known about her audience. These real estate executives had not only survived some extremely difficult business cycles in New York City, but despite many difficulties were among the most successful real estate firms in the country. The consultant should have found this out before the meeting. Then she would have realized that since her audience was a group of aggressive real estate professionals, her remarks needed to be tough, hard-hitting, and above all, short and specific. This group had come to hear the facts—and they wanted to hear them in a hurry.

Here are some ways to get to know an unfamiliar audience:

1. If you are meeting with participants from another company, read published industry reports, such as those of Dun & Bradstreet, which discuss the company.

2. Read magazine articles that cover the professional nature of the group or type of industry in *The Wall Street Journal, Business Week, Forbes, The New York Times,* or the *Institutional Investor.*

3. Ask the people who have invited you for background material that will help you know them.

4. Obtain internal publications, annual reports, orientation programs, and memoranda that describe the views of the people who will attend the meeting.

5. Check with the person arranging the meeting to learn:

    a. The size of the audience—two or two hundred?
    b. The average age of the group—young, middle-aged, or elderly?
    c. The meeting participants' interest and attitude toward your topic—are they deeply interested in the subject, moderately interested, irritated, or threatened?

Often an audience feels uncomfortable with the information you will discuss because it may signal danger to them in terms of their careers or lives. President Carter once faced this problem when addressing civil service workers in Virginia. He let them know that in his view the civil service should be allowed to fire people.

EVEN IF I KNOW WHO ALL THE PARTICIPANTS ARE— HOW WILL I REMEMBER WHO THEY ARE?

Do you remember names and faces? This is one of the biggest problems all of us have, especially at meetings.

Here are five ways to overcome this problem:

1. Listen for the exact name and title of each person when you shake hands. If this is not made clear, ask the participant to repeat his or her name, ask for a business card, or when appropriate, write down the person's name.

2. Set up a seating chart for the meeting. If it is a small group, outline the shape of the table and the arrangement of chairs and write down the names and titles of each person at the meeting.

3. Associate the names you hear with someone or something familiar. Upon meeting Neil Glenn, think of John Glenn, the former astronaut and current U.S. senator.

4. If it is a large group, provide tent cards and a marker and ask all participants to write their name and title on a card.

5. During the meeting, address individuals by name to reinforce your learning.

EVEN IF I REMEMBER NAMES, HOW DO I KNOW HOW TO ADDRESS PEOPLE?

The best way to address people is by their first name, regardless of age and experience level, except when you are specifically directed to do otherwise. For example: The president of the United States, heads of state, governors, senators, congressmen, judges, some academicians, and some medical doctors generally prefer to be addressed by title.

Consider the sexual makeup of the group: The speaker can often offend by singling out an audience member with a comment such as "Thank you, gentlemen and our one lovely lady."

When the speaker is much younger than the listeners, the age difference might also warrant the use of a title. Otherwise, Dr. Wayne Dyer in his book, *Pulling Your Own Strings*, says that addressing people by their first names tends to make them feel more comfortable and establishes a one-on-one relationship.

SUMMARY

All meetings have in them people who desire recognition of their needs. There may be as few as two or as many as several hundred, depending on what the meeting is about. The more you know about them—age, social and economic background, motivation, and experience—the more successful you will be in meeting the needs of your participants. Complete the following "Know Your Audience Checklist." If you answer "no" to any of the questions, take the necessary steps to change the answer to "yes." Retest your expected outcomes. If all signs are go (no "no" 's), move ahead with your meeting.

As illustrated in the retirement example, you may need two meetings; or as in the example of the management consultant who spoke to the real estate executives, you may need to select a new desired outcome.

KNOW YOUR AUDIENCE CHECKLIST

	YES	NO

- Do I know how many participants there will be?
- Do I know the expectations of the group?
- Do I know the experience level of the group?
- Do I know the motivation of the group?
- Do I know the social and economic background of the group?
- Do I know the sexual makeup of the group?

PREPARE
YOUR AGENDA

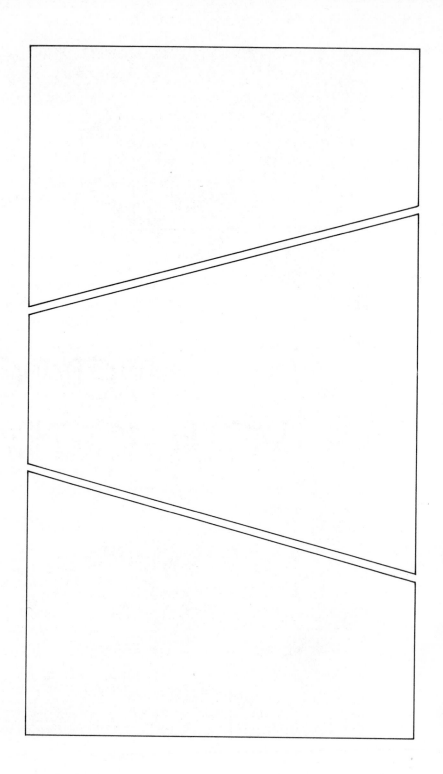

An agenda is an essential part of any successful meeting. It should be carefully constructed so that it reads like a "who-done-it" mystery backwards. It is your strongest defense against a meeting that takes on an unexpected character.

Before we go into the particulars of putting together an agenda, consider these tips:

1. Keep the agenda short—one page only.

2. If possible, send copies of the agenda ahead of the meeting and indicate that participants may submit suggestions for additions and revisions.

3. Use the agenda to introduce the meeting, to allow everyone to settle down and get to work.

4.   An agenda always answers these four questions:

What?
Who?
Where?
When?

WHEN DO YOU PREPARE AN AGENDA?

Research has shown that most people prepare an agenda before they identify the purpose, outcomes, resources, and attendees required for their meeting. We have found that the best agenda is developed after the purpose, outcome, resources, and attendees have been determined. If you start with the agenda before considering these other items, you:

- Tend to forget to determine the real purpose and desired outcome

- Develop time blocks that are fixed and inflexible

- Put the focus on the low-priority items

Let's look at an example of this faulty agenda preparation pattern.

A group of bank managers were to meet with the chairman of the board. They hoped to gain approval for a complex loan to a large client. After months of research and endless meetings with the client, they felt the bank should be the sole source of a large loan. They felt prepared. They know their audience. At the meeting, the chairman rejected their proposal.

In an informal discussion following the meeting, the meeting process was reviewed in detail. The specific purpose was to determine why the meeting failed to achieve the desired outcome.

The group reached the following conclusions:

- Although they had an agenda, they had not discussed what they should do if the chairman objected to their proposal.

- They had failed to discuss the needs and expectations of the chairman.

- They had failed to "dry-run" their new idea against those of their colleagues who were committed to existing banking policy.

Their meeting would have been more successful had they spent time identifying the chairman's expectations and needs. They would have then proposed an agenda outlining a joint financing venture well within the bank's loan policies.

In the meeting planning process the agenda is the last thing you create. An agenda is to meeting planning what dessert is to dinner.

How to organize an agenda is described below.

HOW DO YOU ORGANIZE AN AGENDA?

The first step to organizing an agenda is to simply list every item you wish to cover at the meeting. Then reorganize your list in one of the following three formats:

1.   *A Chronological List*

Rearrange the items on the list chronologically if they so lend themselves.

2.   *A Priority List*

Arrange topics to be discussed in the order of importance.

3.   *A Time-Sensitive List*

List first those topics thought to require the most discussion time.

The purpose of your meeting will enable you to decide whether to use a chronological, priority, or time-sensitive organization of specific agenda items.

Many meetings require the topics to be organized in chronological order so that the meeting attendees understand the relative importance of the items to be discussed. An example of a chronological agenda follows on page 43. It was developed for a meeting before the board of directors of Marsh & McLennan, Incorporated, to explain the need for a professional development program. The agenda seemed to work. The directors discussed all points outlined as they were listed.

Some successful meeting planners agree that it is useful to put the agenda together in order of importance. Others choose to arrange items so that "minor items" can be taken care of at the beginning of the meeting, then moving to more important topics. The latter approach is problematic: Time management specialists have noted that the larger items are rarely addressed adequately because the trivia takes longer than expected. People get fatigued and leave before the significant items are discussed.

> For example, at a finance meeting the setting up of budgets for three major human resources activities was deferred until the end of the day to give the meeting participants an opportunity to study the previous quarter's expenses. By the time the finance committee was ready to discuss these items, it was after 6 p.m. The committee convened again three months later. In the meantime, the human resources projects never got off the ground—a decision, many felt, that caused a 20% increase in staff turnover.

The most important topics don't always take the most time to discuss.

PROPOSAL
PROFESSIONAL DEVELOPMENT PROGRAM
OPERATING COMMITTEE
July 24, 1979

AGENDA

TIME	TOPIC	SPEAKER
9:00	The Purpose of a Professional Development Program	Harold Jones
9:15	An Overview of the Professional Development Program	Pamela Schneider

A. *Why* a Professional Development Program?

B. *Why* Develop Our Own Professional Development Program?

C. *Whom* will the Program Address?

D. *What* Kinds of Courses Will Be Developed?

E. *What* Sequence of Courses Will Be Developed?

F. *How* Will the Courses Be Developed?

- Phases of Development
- Course Enrollment Procedures
- Course Costs

G. Benefits

H. Recommendations

10:00	Discussion	
10:45	Summary	

A member attended a board meeting of the Financial Women's Association of New York where the most important item under discussion was the implementation of a plan to use an outside resource to handle all administrative plans. This was one of the most significant and cost-demanding acts of the organization, yet the discussion and subsequent vote took less than three minutes because of prior meetings and agreements among members.

WHO WILL ATTEND THE MEETING?

A rule to follow when deciding who should be at a meeting is:

IT IS BETTER TO INCLUDE THAN TO EXCLUDE.

Since information about upcoming meetings travels fast in organizations, consider carefully who should be invited to participate. When there is a gray area regarding whether or not to invite an individual, we suggest erring in favor of inviting rather than excluding.

If the purpose of a meeting is to provide information or to ask people to vote on a previously discussed issue, size presents no barrier. However, when the topics under consideration require thorough analysis and synergistic decision making, invite only six or seven individuals.

Once you believe that your list of meeting attendees is complete, double check that all are listed on the memorandum describing the agenda. We recall a horror story when the members of the board of a major corporation were invited to a planning session. However, the names of two of the directors were inadvertently left off the memo describing the session. This oversight could have caused a loss of credibility even before the meeting started. However, fortunately, the error was caught before the memorandum was issued.

WHAT SHOULD THE AGENDA SAY ABOUT WHERE THE MEETING IS BEING HELD?

When making up the list of attendees, follow a consistent format. If you list all men as Mr., list all women as Ms. If you use initials for some people, use them for all, as people are sensitive to these details. It is probably safest to list attendees in alphabetical order. People want to know why they have been invited to a meeting, and they want to know who else will be there and why. The agenda should answer these questions.

You'll also want to provide a paragraph or two in the agenda explaining why each person has been invited to attend as well as the contribution each person is expected to make.

Here are four simple rules to follow:

1. Provide as many specifics as possible.
2. Provide a telephone number to be used as a message center.
3. Describe appropriate dress.
4. Describe the availability of resources.

Now let's take a look at each of these four rules:

1.　*Provide as Many Specifics as Possible.*

This is essential. If, for example, there are out-of-town guests, provide a map or directions of how to get from the airport to the meeting site. Even if the meeting site is a familiar location, be sure to clarify the specifics for all the participants.

A memorandum was sent to the chairman of the board of a major company telling him to come to the company training center for a Friday question-and-answer session with management trainees. When he finally arrived that morning, he was furious. The memorandum neglected to include the fact that the meeting was on the fifth floor, not the sixth. He had just wasted twenty minutes getting on and off elevators trying to discover on what floor the session was being held.

2.   *Provide a Telephone Number to Be Used as a Message Center.*

To avoid frequent telephone interruptions during a meeting, provide in the agenda the phone number where all calls will be answered for meeting participants. Also make it clear that only emergency calls will be put through to the meeting room.

3.   *Describe Appropriate Dress.*

Should the agenda outline dress requirements? Yes. Where a meeting is held often indicates how participants should dress. For example, cities usually dictate business dress; a resort site, casual clothes.

Dress does affect a meeting. For instance, even when a meeting is in the office, indicating normal business attire, put a note in the agenda which says something like: "Since this will be a demanding meeting, feel free to remove your jacket and roll up your sleeves to work." Or when a meeting is held at a conference center, you may wish to state in your agenda memorandum that informal attire is in order.

One speaker, who was to address a meeting of 500 financial executives in Orlando, noted that whereas the participants were dressed in Bermuda shorts and slacks, each of the speakers on the platform wore a jacket and tie. Furthermore, all the guest speakers were fully attired in suits and ties. What happened? The participants were sent a memo indicating that attire should be informal; unfortunately, the speakers were not given the same information. The speaker admitted, after giving his talk, that he felt very uncomfortable on the plat-form. He also felt that his out-of-place formality affected his talk.

Now ask yourself:

HAVE I TOLD THE MEETING PARTICIPANTS WHAT THEY MUST DO TO PREPARE FOR THE MEETING?

Here are some tips that will make participant prework more palatable and more likely to be completed:

1. Indicate the amount of time any articles or memoranda should take to read.

2. Identify certain key questions and ask the reader to answer them before the meeting.

3. Explain why prestudy will benefit the participants and help ensure a smooth meeting.

Everyone takes meeting preparation much more seriously if they know, for example, that they will have to vote on a resolution. People are often most strongly motivated to attend a meeting when they know they will participate in the development of a final product or package. The agenda could read something like:

- "Be prepared to vote on the following resolution. . . ."

- "Since we will develop and finalize the list of speakers for this year's events, please read through the attached list and be prepared to present your ideas."

- "Bear in mind that we will make no final decisions at this meeting but will continue to explore the issues involved at future meetings."

DID I DESCRIBE THE AVAILABILITY OF RESOURCES?

If meeting participants will give reports, state in the agenda that the meeting room will have chalkboard and chalk, flipchart and markers, a slide carousel and screen, and so forth.

People also like to know if the site has recreational facilities and what they are. Are there stores close by? How about restaurants? Include this information in your agenda as well. Your participants will appreciate it.

Another seemingly simple idea to present in an agenda is:

WHAT SHOULD THE AGENDA SAY ABOUT WHEN THE MEETING WILL BE HELD AND HOW LONG IT WILL LAST?

All agendas must describe:

Day

Date

Year

Time—a.m. or p.m.

Concluding time

For example, "We will meet on Tuesday, July 5, 1980, from 2 to 4 p.m. in the East Conference Room on the 12th floor." Some planners believe that this much detail is unnecessary. Certainly, it may not be needed for notification purposes; however, it is vital for historical records.

Certain times are better than others for calling a meeting. People usually arrive late for a 9 a.m. meeting because of commuter problems. End-of-day meetings cause a similar problem because a previous meeting or phone call can delay people.

In the agenda, mention the need to be prompt. Often a statement like: "Please arrive on time. We will need the full two hours to discuss the following topics" helps to motivate people to arrive on time. This also lets people know how long the meeting is scheduled to last.

Also useful is a phrase such as: "Please be sure your return travel arrangements are not scheduled before 6 p.m. so that we will have the full allotted time for our work." Such a statement reduces people's tendency to leave early.

Most people prefer a two- or three-day conference during the middle or at the end of the week, so that the beginning of the week can be used to get their office and staff in order. When planning a day-long meeting, remember the "Rule of Reasonable Length." After ninety minutes, schedule a fifteen-minute break. Day-long meetings need breaks to keep participants alert and productive.

When you invite outside speakers to address a group, position them according to the length of the meeting. In other words, in a week-long program, the worst place for a guest speaker is Thursday afternoon. Participants are tired and less willing to accept an "intruder." The best place is either at the beginning of the week, Monday morning, after the 10:15 coffee break; or Friday morning.

All right, now you have organized your list of topics and you have stated what you expect to occur at the meeting. You also know who will attend the meeting and where it will be held and how long it will last. Now consider this question:

HAVE I ALLOWED FOR FLEXIBILITY IN MY AGENDA?

You can achieve flexibility through these techniques:

- Ask the recipients to submit suggestions or revisions to your meeting plan.

- Put realistic time frames next to each item to be discussed.
- Set aside sufficient time for telephone and stretch breaks.

When you build an agenda that requires you to:

1.   Consider *how to organize* your agenda

2.   Consider what the *outcome of the meeting* should be and state it

3.   Describe participant meeting *preparation*

4.   Allow for *flexibility*

you have produced a superior agenda.

A sample agenda follows.

Date: May 22, 1983

From: Pamela J. Schneider

To: Joe. H. Brown
           Lawrence L. Dean
           Norbert D. Foster
           Martin McNulty
           Nicholas R. Masters
           Harold S. Tanner
           Robert J. Turner
           James J. Wilnot
           Evelyn A. Wolton

Subject: July 21 and 22, 1983, Professional Development Committee Meeting

I look forward to joining you at our July 21 and 22, 1983, Professional Development Committee meeting to be hosted by Area 10. Confirmed July 21 hotel reservations have been made for you at the Four Seasons Hotel, 2800 Pennsylvania Avenue, N.W. Washington, D.C., 202-342-0444.

We will meet at 7:30 p.m. for dinner at the "F" Street Club, 1925 F Street, N.W., Washington, D.C., 202-331-1925, on July 21. The meeting will be held on July 22 at the Four Seasons.

Detailed below is our agenda.

July 21, 1983 7:30 p.m.	Cocktails and Dinner "F" Street Club Guest Speaker: William S. Stone Senior Vice President and Head, Area 10 "Long-Range Plans for Area 10: How Does Professional Development Fit In?"
July 22, 1983 9 a.m.	Client Training Target Audience: Financial Executives

- Topic Outline
- Developers and Instructors
- Locations
- Dates
- Marketing
  - Account Executives
  - Financial Executive Institute
  - Press
- Pricing

Target Audience: Risk Management Novitiates

- Topic Outline
- Developers and Instructors
- Locations
- Dates
- Marketing
  - Account Executives
  - RIMS
  - Press
- Pricing

10:30 a.m.	L. F. DeNess—Legal Education Needs—P/D

12:00   Luncheon: The Four Seasons
                            Discussion: Use of Video at M&M

1 p.m.   1983 Course Schedule

                            1. Possible New Courses
                               • Political Risk
                               • Claims
                               • Office Head Management
                               • Industry Briefings
                            2. Scheduling of Existing Courses
                            3. Prerequisites, Required Courses, and Grade-
                               Level Requirements
                            4. P/D Committee 1982 Assignment:

2:30 p.m.   Local Office Training
                            Meeting—October 1983

                                  Agenda
                                  -Course descriptions
                                  -Counseling procedures
                                  -Administration
                                  -Work plan (example)
                                  -Budget

3:30 p.m.   Update On Current Courses

                               • Cash Flow and Emerging—Evelyn Wolton
                               • Creativity—Nick Masters
                               • Multinational—Had Tanner
                               • Managing New Business Developers—
                                 Robert J. Turner/Joe H. Brown
                               • M&M III—Larry Dean
                               • Industry Briefings—Larry Dean
                               • Electric Marshland—Nick R. Masters
                               • Captives—Evelyn Wolton

5 p.m.   Close

Please read Len DiNapoli's and Jay Lewis' memos (attached) and be prepared to comment on them.

PJN:er

cc: William S. Stone
    Leonard F. DeNess
    Lorne V. Palmer
    Guy Minter
    Professional Development Cabinet
    Sally E. Greenwold

SUMMARY

When planning your meeting, remember that the agenda is the final product—not the first step—of your meeting planning. As such it contains all the information that will enable the participant to come to the meeting prepared. Keep it flexible by reviewing it with the participant before the meeting. It should be a road map for the meeting, not a stone wall or obstacle for producing effective results.

When a meeting planner thinks through these questions before preparing an agenda, the meeting is off to a head start:

1. What is this meeting about?

2. Who will attend the meeting?

3. Where is this meeting being held?

4. When and for how long is the meeting?

Once you have written your agenda, use this checklist to assure that these all-important items have been included.

AGENDA
CHECKLIST

	YES	NO

- Identified one main issue to be discussed at the meeting

- Wrote a general outline for the meeting

- Thought through who should attend the meeting

- Thought through *why* the meeting topic is of importance to each meeting member

- Arranged each item on the agenda in order of importance

- Made sure that each item on the agenda is time bound

- Scheduled sufficient time to discuss each part of the topic

- Included time for breaks in the agenda and scheduled a break every hour and a half

- Clearly assigned responsibility for a given topic

SELECTING YOUR MEETING LOCATION

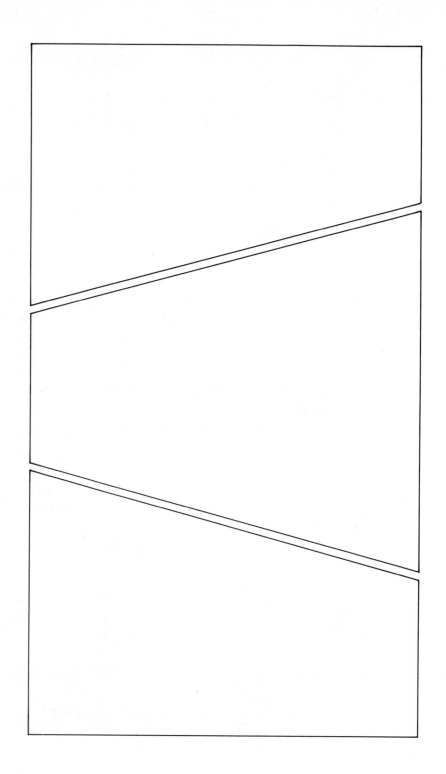

T he success of any meeting depends on the environment created by the place where the meeting is held. That's why it is so important for the person in charge of planning the meeting to ask these questions:

- Where should I hold this meeting?
- What should the meeting facilities offer?
- What should be the layout for the meeting room?

Let's take a look at each of these questions:

WHERE SHOULD I HOLD THIS MEETING?

On-Site Meetings

There are advantages and disadvantages for every site selected. When weighing these, you should consider an on-site meeting room. The advantages of on-site meetings are:

- Convenience
- Accessibility of related materials and people
- Cost

Offsetting these advantages are several disadvantages. They are:

- Telephone interruptions
- Drop-in visitors
- The general background flow of day-to-day activities

These disadvantages can seriously distract participants from the meeting agenda.

Off-Site Meetings

At a client task force meeting, the leader suggested that the task force be held in a conference facility instead of in the client's own luxurious meeting room. The leader pointed out that there is a psychological advantage to renting another room for the meeting. The participants believe that their presence at a meeting matters if they are being sent out of the office to attend it.

Off-site locations set a tone and establish an atmosphere that should help you achieve the purpose of your meeting. Before you select an off-site location, visit it. It is always best to see for yourself, since your selection involves not only cost, but the total effectiveness and impact of your meeting.

Conference center facilities are in.business to run seminars and meetings and can provide for the unique requirements of each group. Such facilities usually have complete hotel accomodations. They have fully equipped meeting rooms as well as experienced staff able to accommodate all speaker audiovisual needs as well as to service any areas of concern during the meeting.

The disadvantages of off-site locations are:

- The location will probably not be centrally located or conveniently located for all.
- Commuting inconvenience can offset the time requirements of the meeting.

When there is a psychological need to create a feeling of comfort, as part of the meeting, a restaurant can be a very useful meeting place. Restaurants are probably the most commonly used off-site locations for business meetings in the United States.

The person in charge of the meeting must accept the responsibility for both managing the service and paying the check, so that this does not encumber the work that has to be accomplished.

Restaurants may be conducive to meetings where:

- A number of team decisions need to be made and the group is not yet acting as a team
- The participants at the meeting need an opportunity to get to know each other
- People have busy work schedules

Restaurant meetings present some distinct advantages. A meeting held at a restaurant lasts only as long as it takes for the meal because waiters tend to hover when you have stayed too long. Holding a meeting at a restaurant tends to break down barriers of formality. Participants engage in small talk as they read their menus and make their selections. Although restaurants have the advantage of removing people from phones and interruptions, they have a very distinct disadvantage—they are often quite noisy. These disadvantages can be overcome by making a careful restaurant selection.

Avoid an intimate, faddish, or stuffy setting. In most instances a bar is also inappropriate for a business meeting. On the other hand, to some a health food restaurant may appear frivolous. Where, then, do you go?

Select a restaurant where you can talk comfortably and have little waiting time for seating and service. Consider joining a luncheon club in your area or use your company's corporate private dining facilities. Establish patronage in a good restaurant so that you get choice seating and service.

Men usually feel that they should pay for lunch. However, the rule in business is that whoever initiated the luncheon pays, regardless of sex.*

Should you drink at lunch? No moral judgments, please! But . . . if you are going to drink, avoid heavy liquor. Keep it light. Stay in control so that your business luncheon meeting will be successful.

One question will help you to decide whether to hold a meeting in your own facility or off-site: What are our time constraints? If you have only a little time, hold the meeting in your own offices. If time permits, seriously consider the advantages of an off-site location.

Use this "Meeting Location Checklist" to help you readily see the options you have.

---

*You can overcome resistance by making it clear at the beginning of the luncheon that you will pay. Then, when the check comes, have your credit card or cash in hand. Sometimes, men will still insist on picking up the tab when with a woman. Avoid a scene: Let the man pick up the tab. Reciprocate by sending a thank-you note.

MEETING LOCATION CHECKLIST

SITE	ADVANTAGES	DISADVANTAGES
1. Place where meeting participants work	a. Convenient b. Access to reference materials and people c. Cost	a. Interruptions b. Distractions c. Meeting not viewed as seriously as one held off-site
2. Conference centers	a. Well managed when run well b. For all-day or several-day meetings c. Psychological lift for participants	a. Expensive b. Inconvenient c. Aggravating when ill-managed
3. Restaurants	a. Creates informality b. Work can be accomplished during meal c. Limits meeting time	a. Limits time b. Encourages small talk c. Encourages distractions d. Noisy

HOW SHOULD I SET UP THE ROOM?

The actual setup of chairs and tables and visual aids contributes to the success of a meeting. The room should be "ready for work" when the participants arrive since this has a tremendous psychological impact on the participants.

A meeting leader described to us how important room setup was to him when he used a meeting facility just outside Houston. He had set up an elongated "U" arrangement of tables and chairs.

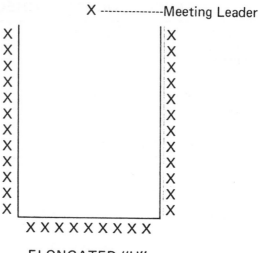

ELONGATED "U"

During the meeting the leader realized that this setup was causing many problems: First, there were air conditioners in the back of the room, which made it impossible for people in the back to hear what was being said. Second, every time the seminar speaker moved into the group not only did he lose eye contact but he could not be heard by the participants seated in the front of the room. After the meeting, the leader met with the setup people and asked for a different room to accommodate his arrangement. When his meeting convened the next morning, it had been relocated to a room better constructed for effective listening and eye contact. He used a participatory setup:

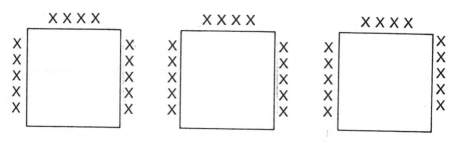

PARTICIPATORY SET UP

Nine basic room arrangements are shown in the chart on page 64. Before meeting, use this chart to select the arrangement that best suits your speaker, the number of participants, and your purpose.

ROOM SETUPS

WHAT DO I NEED TO CONSIDER WHEN SETTING UP THE MEETING ROOM?

A friend of ours was once asked to give a presentation in a lovely facility just outside Philadelphia. The person who invited her proudly showed her the room where she would be speaking. The room had a large picture window with a magnificent view of stables and horses. She realized immediately that no matter how interesting her talk was, the meeting participants would be more interested in seeing the horses than in listening to what she had to say. She explained this to her host, and he agreed that the curtains could be closed during the meeting.

When setting up a meeting room, review the basics:

1. Consider the room size and the number of people it will accommodate. People tend to feel uncomfortable if there are few people in a large room. By the same token, an overcrowded room makes everyone feel claustrophobic.

2. Find out where the light switches are and if they will suit the purposes of the meeting.

3. If slides are to be used, check to see if the room can be darkened without blackening it, so that the participants can continue to take notes during the presentation.

4. Find out if the meeting room has a window with draperies that close.

ROOM SET UP	ADVANTAGES*	DISADVANTAGES*

1. Classroom

xxxxxxxxx
xxxxxxxxx
xxxxxxxxx

x-Leader

a. Allows for many people
b. Leader is clearly in charge

a. Encourages one-way communication
b. Encourages side-bar conversations
c. Hard to hear in back of room

2. U Shape

x -Leader

a. Convenient for 6-20 people
b. Easy for leader to have eye contact with all

a. Discourages small-group team building
b. Reduces getting to know other people
c. Limits movement of leader

3. Participatory

x-Leader

a. Builds teams
b. Easy for leader to move about

a. Increases side-bar conversations
b. Requires wide room

4. Herringbone

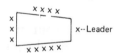

x-Leader

a. Allows use of tables for many people
b. Creates center aisle

a. Hard to hear in back of room
b. Creates impersonal mood

5. Circle

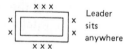

x-Leader

a. Hard to select a leadership position
b. Good morale for people

a. Hard to select a leadership position

6. Rectangle

x x x x

Leader--x

x
x

x x x x x

a. Good for staff meetings
b. Leader can assert control in front of room

a. Limits number of people to size of table
b. Encourages discussion

7. Focused Rectangle

x x x x
x
x   x--Leader
x
x x x x x

a. Creates leadership position
b. Allows for more people than rectangle

a. Creates distance between leader and group

8. Doughnut

x x x
x   x   Leader
x   x   sits
x x x   anywhere

a. Equalizes status of group members
b. Easy to see everyone

a. Limits number of people to size of doughnut

9. Office/Desk

x
x   x--Leader

a. Creates authority
b. Allows intimacy

a. Can be seen threatening

---

*Advantages and disadvantages may be reversed depending on the perception of leader.

WHAT SHOULD I DO ABOUT VISUAL AIDS?

We will not cover the subject of visual aids in detail in this book, but we do believe that visual aids add to the impact of a meeting. Consequently, the information that follows is intended to remind you of the importance of visual aids and to give you a few hints on when to use them. Slide presentations are effective, particularly if kept to ten and no more than fifteen minutes. Basic content slides also help to highlight important information. In a highly technical presentation, include "relief" slides. Relief slides may be humorous or they may make reference to a suitable example that supports the information presented.

The American Society for Training and Development has over three hundred general subject slides. For more information about these slides, contact the American Society for Training and Development, P.O. Box 5307, Madison, WI 53705, 608-274-3440.

Regardless of the nature of the meeting, movies and video tape also help establish a mood and set the pace for the meeting. There are a number of short films and video tapes, two, five, and ten minutes in length, available from Bosustow Productions. Write for a catalog to Bosustow Productions, 1649 11th Street, Santa Monica, CA 90404.

You may also wish to video tape record your meeting. A meeting leader can then use the tape to debrief the meeting by playing it back at a later date. If you decide to use video tape, however, tell the participants why you are taping the meeting and how the tape will be used. Often, taping can totally unnerve people and end spontaneous participation.

Use an overhead projector and transparencies to:

- Display technical problems and information
- List items for discussion

Clear, boldly lettered, hand-made transparencies are generally much more visible than typed transparencies and they are often more legible than flipcharts.

Flipcharts allow a meeting leader to:

- Post the agenda

- Create opportunities for leadership among the participants by allowing them to write items on the flipchart

- Remove ownership of ideas from individuals by placing the ideas on the flipchart

- Create a visual history of the meeting when hung on the meeting room wall

- Provide a mechanism for developing minutes and follow-up task sheets

Blackboards are invaluable when creating flowcharts or organization charts due to their large writing surface. Since items can be easily erased, modifications or suggestions from participants can be included.

SUMMARY

When selecting the location for your meeting, think about the climate or environment you need to achieve your purpose. In some cases, to avoid interruptions you may want to hold the meeting away from the workplace. The cost advantages of an in-house meeting may be outweighed by your desire to meet the expectations and needs of the meeting participants.

Regardless of where the meeting is held—in house, at a conference center, or at a restaurant—a careful review of the meeting room setup will help achieve the desired results. If you need visual aids—flipcharts or slides—to support your major topic, a restaurant may not be an appropriate location. Completing the "Site Selection Checklist" will assist you in avoiding some common pitfalls in site selection. Use this checklist to assure that the site selected satisfies all your requirements before your meeting begins.

SITE SELECTION CHECKLIST

	YES	NO
• Is the size of the room suitable for the number of meeting participants?		
• Are the chairs in the room appropriate? Are they comfortable?		
• Are temperature controls visible?		
• Is there someone available to help set up the room?		
• Do I know where the light switches are?		
• Do I have adequate light sockets and extension cords?		
• Is there space to hang up completed wall charts?		
• Are there drapes that close on the windows?		
• Does the room provide clear views for visual aids?		
• Is the room located away from kitchens, hallways, and coffee-break areas?		

THOSE
ALL IMPORTANT
FIRST FEW
MINUTES

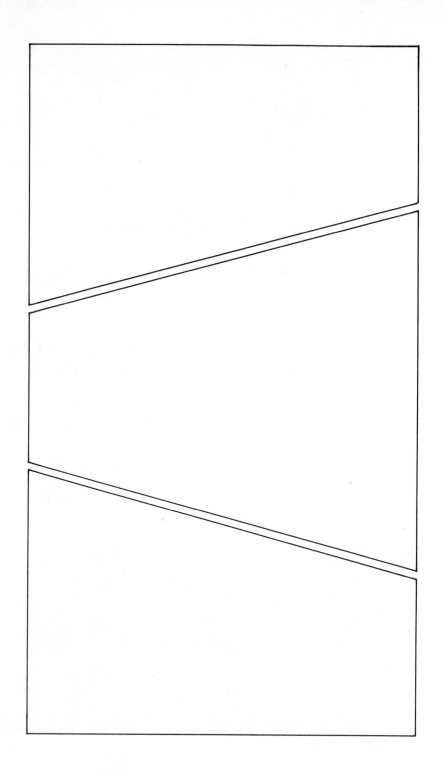

A group of five executives met to hear a consultant review the results of a six-month, in-depth analysis his firm had recently completed of the corporation's data processing operations. Even though the cost of the study was substantial, the results could not only dramatically affect the way the organization did business but save the company a hundred times as much in increased efficiency. As the consultant began his review, he noticed that there was considerable tension in the room, due, he suspected, to both the questions asked during the study and the suspicion that there would be both a reduction of the work force as well as a change in job status among those who were seated before him if his data processing conclusions were implemented.

The consultant sensed the group's tension. He began by using the first few minutes of his presentation wisely. He described how helpful each person in the room had been to his firm's research during the past six months. Then he suggested that everyone take notes or record questions, so that the meeting would not become one where they listened and he talked. The meeting would be a *discussion* of his findings.

This consultant knew the first rule for conducting a successful meeting:

MAKE PEOPLE FEEL COMFORTABLE.

By involving the group, by assuring them they had contributed to the consultant's report, he built allegiance and commitment to the comments he was about to make.

"And don't forget the little pads, in case one of them has an idea."

(Drawing by Gardner Rea, © 1953, The New Yorker Magazine, Inc.)

This vignette illustrates how crucial it is to get a meeting off to the right start. Research in the behavioral sciences indicates that the impact of "the beginning" of any incident, such as school, dating, a first job, or even a meeting, has an enormous effect on the way an individual both perceives the event and remembers it.

In the book, *Contact: The First Four Minutes*, by Leonard Zunin, M.D., the author suggests that the first four minutes of any business or social event have more impact on the attitude of the individuals involved than at any other time during the meeting.

To get your meeting off to the right start, begin before the meeting convenes. Use the "Advanced Preparation Checklist" at the end of this chapter to assist you in reviewing your preparation for the meeting.

Arrive about an hour early at the meeting room to take care of any details. Check out the arrangement of the room. Refer to the preceding chapter for room layout choices. Make certain that all audiovisual or other necessary equipment is set out. Review the "Site Selection Checklist" on page 67. Have the person in charge of arranging the meeting set up triangular tent cards with each individual's name on both sides of the card. Following is a sample tent card:

Tent cards allow a meeting leader to control who will sit next to whom. This discourages side discussions from occurring. If necessary, pass out name tags as well as note pads and pens or pencils.

You will also have an opportunity to prepare a large, poster-size flipchart or blackboard version of the agenda. The agenda should be:

- Prepared with time frames for each item to be discussed, including time allotted for breaks

- Visible to everyone at the meeting

In addition, distribute typed photocopies of the agenda which match the posted version. You may wish to prepare additional flipcharts which cover technical or related information of the topics to be discussed.

Be present to greet participants as they arrive and make people feel welcome.

As the participants arrive, the meeting leader should shake hands with each person. When shaking hands, remember to:

1. Look the person in the eye

2. Find out his or her name

3. Tell the person your name

4. Thank the person for attending the meeting

5. Indicate where the person:

   a. May hang up his or her coat
   b. Get a cup of coffee
   c. Should sit

When the participants have not previously met, if appropriate, begin a meeting by asking each person to introduce himself or herself. While each person is speaking, draw a room arrangement chart. Note each individual's name and position as he or she is introduced. Now you're ready to begin!

WHAT TO DO WHEN THE FIRST FEW MINUTES ARE SPENT WAITING FOR SOME ATTENDEES

Rule One:

REWARD PUNCTUAL PEOPLE: START ON TIME.

However, use good judgment when implementing Rule One.

If it seems inadvisable to start because too few people have arrived, suggest to those present where they may make phone calls or have a cup of coffee until the meeting formally begins. Then tell them when they should be back in the meeting room. The point is to avoid alienating those who arrive on time.

GUIDELINES FOR RUNNING THE ACTUAL MEETING

The way we talk, walk, gesture, and, of course, dress is a language we use to communicate who we are, what we think of ourselves, and what we want others to think of us.

A leader's appearance is of critical importance. A leader must appear:

1. Well groomed in understated clothing
2. Enthusiastic
3. Open
4. Calm
5. Objective

6. Balanced

7. Friendly

When you speak, use language that communicates:

- Use plain English.
- Avoid jargon.
- Provide definitions to necessary technical terms.

In your opening remarks avoid intonation that is:

1.   Satiric

"Look at all those happy, smiling, enthusiastic faces before me."

2.   Bitter

"I don't know why you people can never bring your agendas with you."

3.   Negative

"We probably shouldn't have held this meeting anyway."

4.   Dull

"The reason I brought you together is . . . ."

Also consider your appearance.

One veteran leader recalled watching a speaker at a major bank give a presentation on the current economic picture of the country. Little did he know that most of the meeting's participants hardly heard a word he was saying. They were trying to figure out what the tiny bear on his tie was supposed to mean.

Jewelry or chains make noise. Turtlenecks on men still create a bohemian impression on some participants. Bright colors or black both tend to overwhelm an audience. Attire that is unsuitable to the environment or could reduce credibility should not be worn.

For example, in a New York bank, a management consultant observed that any man who did not wear a handkerchief in his breast coat pocket and a gold tie bar under the knot of his "rep" tie was at a psychological disadvantage to those who did.

As a manager, every workday requires you to dress as though you were lunching with the chairman of the board. Discreet dresses and suits, pumps, subtle jewelry, and good grooming let people know you're in charge.

The point is: When the participants are thinking about how overdressed or underdressed they are, they are not thinking about the topics under discussion.

The first few minutes of a meeting sets the tone. Each participant should feel welcome—that their presence is valued and that the leader is in control.

As part of your opening remarks, you may say: "I'm delighted to be here." There is a psychological benefit in saying this. The statement relaxes the person saying it because it creates in the individual a good feeling about running the meeting. Although participants generally do not even hear these words, they do sense that the person running the meeting is confident, calm, and in charge. Generally speaking, participants also appreciate it when the leader stands when running the meeting, as this is both a gesture of control and a show of concern for keeping the meeting running smoothly.

DURING THE SECOND FEW MINUTES

Let people know why they are at the meeting and why they should avoid any meeting interruptions.

A most effective way to do this is to prepare a flipchart with the words:

> **Why me?**
> **Why you?**
> **Why now?**

These three little questions are valuable because virtually all people ask themselves:

- Why is the person in front of the room running the meeting?

- Why am *I* sitting here listening to this discussion?

- Why am I here *now* listening to this discussion?

Stating these concerns on a flipchart shows the meeting participant that the leader is sensitive to their concerns.

Now, of course, the leader has to answer those questions. So . . . explain why you are running the meeting. Perhaps you could provide a brief biographical sketch or explain how or why you were put in charge of the meeting.

To answer the question "Why you?," review the purpose for the meeting. Using a "round-robin approach," ask each participant to comment on what will make the meeting valuable for him or her. Note their responses on a flipchart which you can then hang on the wall.

"Why now" is best answered by explaining that the input the participants provide *now* will have an impact on an event in their own and other's lives in the near future.

Once you have reviewed the reasons the leader is in charge, why the individuals are participating, and why the meeting is taking place, refer the participants to the meeting agenda, posted on the wall, and distribute photocopies to them.

Review each item and the time allotted to it.

Also mention the breaks. Explain where the bathrooms, phones, and the message board are and when the meeting will end. Ask that phone calls and interruptions be limited to an "emergency only" basis. Then ask if the participants believe the agenda is complete, satisfactory, and clear. Ask if they are comfortable with the time frames for the breaks and can live with the commitment for when the meeting will end.

Hold to the agenda. You will be able to do this if:

- The agenda reflects input from others
- The agenda is announced
- The agenda is visible

THE THIRD FEW MINUTES

During the third few minutes the leader asks specific individuals in the room to:

1. Take minutes. The person assigned this responsibility is the secretary of the meeting.

2. Keep track of the time. The person assigned this responsibility will be the "gatekeeper."

3. Assure that individuals who are assigned responsibilities

accomplish them. This person is the "follow-up manager."

These roles create greater involvement for the participants since they are an integral part of the meeting process. Assign these jobs rather than asking for volunteers, as people are frequently either shy or reluctant to assume these responsibilities. Nonetheless, most people are flattered to be asked to do them. During this time, review the "process ground rules" for how you would like the meeting to run. These comments could be appropriate:

"While I make this report, whenever you have questions, please feel free to interrupt me."

"I have allotted time for questions about this report later in the meeting. Please make a note of any questions on the paper provided and ask them then."

"There are several areas where I particularly need your input today."

These "process ground rules" set the stage. They let the participant know:

1. How you want the meeting managed

2. That you are in control of the meeting

3. That the utilization of time has been considered carefully

Generally, the purpose of a meeting is to encourage input, conversation, and discussion of a given topic. To do this effectively, set up a conducive atmosphere. Tell the participants they are welcome to remove their jackets during the meeting, and then remove your jacket.

Research has shown that note taking improves listening, since taking notes is a more active listening process than simply sitting and hearing passively. Participants will get more from the discussion because they can record their ideas as well as any new technical or factual information.

The best way to review any meeting would be to see it on video tape. This way you could see and hear all the action—nonverbal signs and conversational tone as well as the specific information covered. It would be an instant replay of the meeting. However, this is not a readily available tool for most meeting managers. Instead, you must rely on your memory and your notes.

And before we go any further . . .

A FEW WORDS ABOUT TAKING MINUTES

Meeting minutes describe the health of a group meeting in much the same way that clipboard notes describe the health of a patient in a hospital.

Minutes serve as a:

- Permanent record of the meeting
- Record of the accomplishments and plans of the group
- Guide for handling the same or similar situations in the future
- Follow up and evaluation of the progress of action plans

When assigning someone the responsibility to take minutes at a meeting, provide this list of observations:

1. To show the development of a topic, include a statement that shows the continuity of thought as well as the action taken.

2. Do not include confidential statements or personal references.

3. Include the opinions of the minority. This will help to maintain the self-esteem of these individuals and will show them that their opinions were heard.

4. Minutes communicate with absent members, peer groups, and management who should be kept informed.

You may also wish to provide these rules for taking minutes:

1. Minutes should be clear and concise.

2. Include only the information covered in the meeting.

3. The wording of a decision agreed to at the meeting is never changed.

4. The secretary must sign the minutes of the meeting under the heading "Respectfully Submitted."

5. Supplementary information is sent under separate cover.

Here is an example of a format for meeting minutes that works well. Use it as a guide.

AN EXAMPLE OF MEETING MINUTES

MEMBERSHIP COMMITTEE

Minutes of Meeting: *August 7, 1979*

MEMBERS IN ATTENDANCE:

Carole Jones	Elizabeth Heller
Marie Smith	Jennie Kintini
Joyce Javis	Anne Martin

NEXT MEETING:

Tuesday, September 11, 1979—5:30 p.m.
280 Park Avenue South
7th floor Conference Room

NEW MEMBERS ACCEPTED:

Anita Millot
Federal Home Loan Bank Board
1700 G Street N.W.
Washington, D.C. 20520
202-377-6590
Board Member

Lynn Newman
Corporate Finance
Bache Halsey Stuart Shields, Inc.
100 Gold Street
New York NY 10038
212-791-1000

Susan Bearden
Vice President
Kidder, Peabody & Co., Inc.
10 Hanover Square
New York NY 10005
212-747-2750

Fay Rhinehart
First Vice President
Blyth Eastman Dillon & Co., Inc.
1221 Avenue of the Americas
New York NY 10028
212-730-4880

Mary Rossman
Assistant Vice President
Citibank, N.A.
399 Park Avenue
New York NY 10043
212-687-7420

Dr. Mary Teale
Vice President
Textron, Inc.
40 Westminster Street
Providence RI 02903
401-421-2800

These memebers will be included in the new year's dues solicitation and membership questionnaire.

OUTSTANDING ASSIGNMENTS:

Lydia Lynch   to Joyce Javis
Renata von Steffan   to Joyce Javis
Judy Elford   to Carole Jones
Pamela Swan   to Carole Jones
Irma Rostein   to Jennie Kintini
Evelyn Fastin   to Marie Smith
Deborah McHill   to Alice Mayfield

APPLICATIONS INCOMPLETE OR TABLED UNTIL NEXT MEETING:

1. Returned to Sponsors: Carol Barry, B.J. Pazicki, Louise Lock

2. Tabled: Beverly Wettenstein, Barbara Pulanski

3. Not qualified—contact Sponsors: Carol Suslow—Joan Ching, Leslie Barnes

MEMBERSHIP COMMITTEE

Minutes—August 7, 1979

ISSUES:

I.   All incomplete applications or letters dated prior to 1979 are being removed from the pending files.

II.   The following procedures were reiterated and will be included in the next Newsletter.

    1. Only members may request application forms. Sponsoring members obtain application form from:
Anita Lands, Executive Director
Financial Women's Association
35 East 72nd Street
New York NY 10021
212-794-9208

    2. The sponsor's letter of recommendation, the *two* seconders' letters of recommendation, and the application form (signed by all four parties) should be returned as a package to Anita Lands.*

    3. Sponsors and seconders must be employed by different organizations. The sponsor and one seconder must have been FWA members for more than one year.

    4. Other than being employed in a financial position, an applicant must have been employed for at least 2 years with an MBA and 4 years without.

    5. Applicant must have attended at least three FWA events.

    * The task of membership applications rests with the sponsors.

III.   Member-Meet-Member Luncheons

St. Bartholomew's has agreed to continue our program and to ask us to join. Jennie Kintini will continue to coordinate this program and will consult on a downtown program.

Respectfully Submitted,

August 7, 1979

PRIOR TO DISCUSSING THE CRITICAL ISSUE

Take a few moments to summarize what has been mentioned in the introduction. Ask the participants if they have any questions. Now you are ready to launch into your first agenda item, the principal reason for the meeting.

SUMMARY

The first few minutes of a meeting have an enormous effect on how participants will perceive the value of a meeting. That is why a meeting leader should review both the content of the meeting and the process used to conduct it. Moreover, each participant should feel comfortable and purposeful.

Once the minutes have been recorded, use this checklist to assure their accuracy.

MINUTES-TAKING CHECKLIST

	YES	NO
• Were the names of all participants present listed?		
• Were the time, date, location, and chairman of the meeting described?		
• Were all agenda items and other items discussed and all decisions reached described?		
• Were participants assigned responsibility for action items and follow-up?		
• Were timetables described?		
• Were the date, time, and location of the next meeting described?		

Advance preparation will ensure success. As part of your preparation you should complete this checklist.

ADVANCED PREPARATION CHECKLIST

	YES	NO

- Have I organized the room to ensure that the setup facilitates meeting discussion, but discourages side discussions?

- Do I have prepared nametags and tent cards for each participant?

- Do I usually start meetings when they are planned to start?

- Have I carefully planned the introduction to the meeting and explained why the members of the audience have been invited?

- Am I prepared, in the first four minutes, to explain the agenda of the meeting?

- Have I included in my opening remarks the fact that minutes will be taken to allow for follow-up and to ensure that everyone remembers agreements reached during the meeting?

- Am I prepared to suggest that participants take notes?

- Do I plan to begin with the principal reason the meeting was called?

- Did I include the fact that as a result of the meeting specific work will be assigned to the meeting participants?

LISTEN TO YOUR AUDIENCE

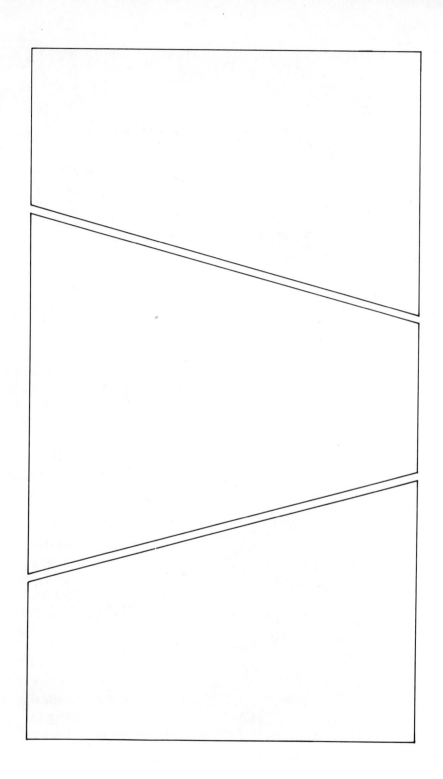

A seasoned financial expert was asked to address a group of 200 women, themselves leaders in the field of finance in the New York City area. The speaker seemed to sense from audience queries, side conversations, and even the women's attitude before the meeting that there was, in the room, hostility toward a man giving women advice in an area in which they considered themselves experts. The speaker should have acknowledged this hostility in the first few minutes of his talk. He didn't. Instead, he ignored it and gave the speech that he planned to give, as if these feelings didn't exist.

During his talk there were constant questions about his information—his facts, statistics, sources. The meeting turned out to be unpleasant for everyone. Why? Because the speaker heard what his audience was saying before the meeting but wasn't really listening. He did not meet the needs of his audience.

Who invited this poor soul to this meeting? The women themselves had. Why were they so hostile? Hadn't they attended the meeting to get information? Because the speaker didn't listen to his audience before the meeting, they focused on *him* rather than on the content of his speech.

Before each meeting ask yourself: "What should I be listening for to achieve the stated purpose of my meeting?" Review this checklist before your next meeting.

WHY LISTEN CHECKLIST

OBJECTIVE	YES	NO
• I want participant(s) to talk freely and frankly.		
• I want this meeting to focus on matters and problems that are important to the participant(s).		
• I want the participant(s) to furnish as much information as possible.		
• I want the participant(s) to get greater insight and understanding of problems as they discuss them.		
• I want the participant(s) to discuss the causes and reasons for problems and identify possible solutions.		
• I want to identify and resolve any sensitive issues.		

LISTENING FOR UNDERSTANDING

Some meeting situations are extremely complex. As you evaluate your need to understand an issue, ask yourself:

"Did I listen to what was being said?"

Before you say "I understand the problem," ask yourself:

"Do I see the whole problem? What, in my experience, enables me to comprehend the issue fully?"

In many cases, we think we understand the problems when in fact we have only a surface knowledge of the details. In reality we may be dealing with symptoms and not causes.

Before a meeting, remind yourself that listening is the key to knowledge and understanding. Have an open mind; you can never know all there is to know.

According to Dr. Albert Mehrabian, noted researcher of listening techniques, if you're not "actively listening," paying attention to both vocal and nonverbal cues, you may miss 93% of what is being said despite the fact that you hear every word.

Whether it's one-on-one or a group meeting, lack of listening is a major barrier to understanding.

How does knowing my audience help me to key my message?

Dr. Robert Hecht, a psychological consultant from New York, has evaluated audience types. He points out that there are basically four types of listeners: the "Forecaster," the "Systemizer," the "Associator," and the "Energizer." Each listening style requires a different presentation approach to reach the receivers.

The accompanying chart, an "Overview of Listener Receptivity Styles," reviews each listener style, focus, and key phrases that each audience type is responsive to hearing. Also listed are professions and occupations to which each style is typically attracted, their time orientation and attention span, environmental cues that identify them, and the presentation approach that should be most effective when speaking to each style. Use this checklist as a reference source so that you'll know how to gear your presentations to your meeting participants. If you don't get through to your audience very early in your presentation, you will either never "get heard" or spend most of your time recovering from a wrong beginning.

OVERVIEW OF LISTENER RECEPTIVITY STYLES*

LISTENER STYLE	PHRASES THEY USE OR LIKE TO HEAR	TYPICAL PROFESSIONS AND/OR OCCUPATIONS	TIME ORIENTATION
FORECASTER	"Here's a new idea." "This has a different twist." "It has never been done before." "Let's look at the big picture." "The long-range implications . . . ."	Research scientists Inventors Academicians Artists Venture capitalists	Long-term future
SYSTEMIZER	"Here's the background." "The evidence is solid." "It's been tested." "Let's start with a dry run." "Here's how it works."	Lawyers Accountants EDP types Engineers	Immediate past/present/ near future
ASSOCIATOR	"I've got a gut feeling." "I have a sixth sense about this." "Name someone influential who has done this." "How we do it matters as much as what we do."	Personnel officers Psychologists Entrepreneurs Bankers Salespersons Insurance agents	Past
ENERGIZER	"What's the bottom line?" "Let's get going." "I only have 2 minutes." "What is the cost/benefit?" "Spare me the details."	Production manager Consultants Stockbrokers Athletes Expediters, dispatchers	Now

*Adapted from *Understanding Your Workstyle,* Lee-Hecht & Associates, New York.

OVERVIEW OF LISTENER RECEPTIVITY STYLES*
(Cont.)

ATTENTION SPAN	ENVIRONMENTAL CUES	BEST PRESENTATION APPROACH TO USE
Longest	Little concern for dress Unusual desks and nontraditional offices Messy office: many books, articles, objets d'art Avant garde climate	35mm slide show with music and lights Unusual approaches Clever synergy
Longer	Organized work space Organized in appearance Keeps "To Do" lists Uses directories and detailed reports	Flowcharts and matrices Flipchart presentation done in logical styles: (a) Background (b) Problem (c) Solutions (d) Recommendations
Long	Wears class ring, school tie Much personal memorabilia on desk Traditional surroundings Wears stylish colorful clothing	Frequent references to individuals Frequent mention of examples of how this has been done in other organizations Use of short, 16mm film Dramatic style
Very short	Gadgetry in offices Airline guide in briefcase Sits near door during meetings Often allows interruptions	"Action Steps" first followed by background information in a brief format Short presentation, overhead transparencies Show results, expected outcomes

BARRIERS TO LISTENING

According to Dr. Ralph Nichols, professor of anthropology at the University of Chicago, not listening can be classified into specific habits. The "Listening Habits Checklist" below summarizes the poor habits that Dr. Nichols has identified and offers suggestions for correcting them. Space has also been provided for you to check your most common barriers. Once you have identified them, develop an action plan to "kick the habit."

LISTENING HABITS CHECKLIST*

HABIT	CAUSES	CORRECTIVE ACTION	INVENTORY		
			ALWAYS	*SOMETIMES*	*NEVER*
In-out	Most people think four times as fast as the average person speaks.	Write down whatever you were thinking that caused you to stop listening. This will enable you to recall what you were thinking at that time. Then get right back to listening.			
Red flag	Some words, when we hear them, upset us and we stop thinking: for example, "layoffs," "behind schedule," "strike," etc.	Write the word down. Listen. Is the speaker using this word correctly or adding a new meaning?			

LISTENING HABITS CHECKLIST (Cont.)

HABIT	·CAUSES	CORRECTIVE ACTION	INVENTORY ALWAYS	SOMETIMES	NEVER
Closed mind	We often think there is no reason to listen because we will hear nothing new.	Set an objective to listen to see if in fact the speaker is saying anything new. This will force you to listen.			
Day-dreaming	Frequently, we hear a word or idea that causes us to think of something else.	If you sense, before the meeting, that you have too many other ideas on your mind, don't go to the meeting. If you find your mind wandering during the meeting, note the thought and then concentrate on listening.			
Too technical or complex	You may attend a meeting thinking the topic is too complex or technical for you to understand.	At the meeting, follow the discussion. Prepare before the meeting. Read articles or skim a book on the topic.			
Mind-guarding	You may not want your pet idea, prejudice, or point of	Listen! Find out what the speaker has to say. Get the other side of			

LISTENING HABITS CHECKLIST* (Cont.)

HABIT	CAUSES	CORRECTIVE ACTION	ALWAYS	INVENTORY SOMETIMES	NEVER
	view challenged. You stop listening, become defensive, and even plan a counterattack.	the question. This leads to better understanding and enables you to reply in a calm and reasonable manner.			
Court reporter	You try to record everything said. However, the speaker speaks faster than you can write.	Jot down the key words. Later put them in an outline format.			
Hubbub listening	Distractions are always present in a meeting.	Practice tuning out these distractions and concentrate on what the speaker is saying.			

*Ralph Nichols, Prof. of Anthropology, University of Chicago.

What is listening?

Listening is an art, a skill, a discipline.

What is involved in listening?

To learn how to listen you must make an intellectual,

behavioral, and emotional commitment and follow these three basic rules:

Rule One:

STOP TALKING

Rule Two:

STUDY YOUR AUDIENCE

Look for vocal and nonverbal cues. Is there much coughing? Are people looking at each other or avoiding each other? Are side conversations occurring?

Rule Three:

CONCENTRATE ON WHAT IS BEING SAID

Try not to think about how you will respond.

Take deep breaths, sit comfortably, and if appropriate, take notes. Erase from your vocabulary the thought and words, "Yes, but" since they interrupt someone else's thought.

GOOD LISTENING REQUIRES A POSITIVE ATTITUDE.

RECOMMENDED LISTENING HABITS

Here are six listening habits. As the meeting leader, use them as guides for listening and communicating in a meeting. The challenge is to use them effectively. This requires practice, repetition, and patience. The examples included may assist you in responding to your audience.

LISTENING HABITS*

CLASSIFICATION	BASIC APPROACH	INTENT	EXAMPLES
1. PARAPHRASING	Paraphrase the main idea.	• To indicate you are listening and understand what is said. • To produce additional interaction.	• "Oh, so you believe that . . . ." • "Based on what you've said, I see that you want to . . . ."
2. THOUGHTFUL	Indicate you understand the feeling behind the idea.	• To indicate you sense the feeling about what is said. • To encourage additional information about the idea presented.	• "You seem to feel very strongly about this." • "It seemed unfair to you at the time." • "You felt put down at the meeting."
3. INDIFFERENT	Listen without making a value judgment.	• To show interest. • To get more information.	• "No kidding." • "Say a little more about that." • "That's exciting." • "Then what happened?"
4. INQUIRING	Use the five W's: WHO? WHAT? WHEN? WHERE? WHY?	• To get additional information. • To go below the surface level.	• "Why did you say . . .?" • "What did you think about . . .?" • "When do you plan to . . .?"
5. REASONING	Find out if all sides of a question have been considered.	• To evaluate pros and cons of an idea. • To gather more facts.	• "Tell me what you like about this idea." • "What is your major concern with what you've decided?"
6. SUMMARY	Bring the conversation to a logical break point, to see if more discussion is required.	• To check ideas. • To focus on a problem. • To evaluate progress.	• "As I understand it, then, you want to . . . ." • "Following your initial step, you will . . . ."

*These six habits were adapted from Dr. Robert K. Burns, University of Chicago, Professor Emeritus, Industrial Relations, "Five Listening Techniques."

Through practice, listening will become second nature to you. To assist you in this process, we have provided these tips.

TIPS ON LISTENING

DO	DON'T
• Allow enough time to cover a topic	• Pass judgment too quickly or in advance
• Maintain eye contact	• Argue
• Paraphrase the speaker	• Interrupt
• Nod your head	• Give advice unless requested
• Use silence when silence is appropriate. REMEMBER: *SILENCE GIVES YOU TIME TO LISTEN*	• Jump to conclusions
• Concentrate on finding the problem, not the symptom of the problem	• Lose your temper
• Listen for causes for the problem	• Ask closed questions
• Help the speaker associate the problem with the cause	• Joke when it's inappropriate
• Encourage the speaker to develop an action plan to solve a problem	• Appear cold and indifferent
• Show interest	
• Watch for nonverbal signals	
• Be understanding	
• Express empathy	
• Summarize the discussion	

Your meeting is in progress. To accomplish your stated purpose, ask yourself these questions:

MEETING-IN-PROGRESS CHECKLIST

HAVE I:	YES	NO
• Asked for feedback? *Example:* "What do you think about the new policy?"		
• Made the group feel they own the meeting by allowing each member to contribute?		
• Allowed the group to participate actively in decisions?		
• Addressed the issue of leadership by allowing group members to comment on the meeting process?		
• Rotated the leadership responsibility so everyone has a chance to be in charge?		
• Allowed brief brainstorming sessions during the meeting to see if a particular assumption might be incorrect?		
• Selected a meeting participant to assume the role of devil's advocate?		
• Listened to what is being said?		
• Watched for nonverbal signals?		
• Read nonverbal signals from the group and commented on negative reactions?		

AND SOME PEOPLE DO LISTEN . . .

Dr. Newman, coauthor of this book, once received a letter after she gave a speech.

"You listen like no one I've ever met. You made each one who spoke to you feel as if his or her question was the missing link to the final equation."

Listening is a skill people appreciate.

SUMMARY

Reading the reaction of the group will require you to listen to your audience. Your ability to react to the group's words and vocal intonation will help you adjust the direction of the meeting.

Reviewing your listening habits from time to time prevents you from losing your audience and will help you meet their needs and expectations.

PREPARE FOR A DIFFICULT AUDIENCE

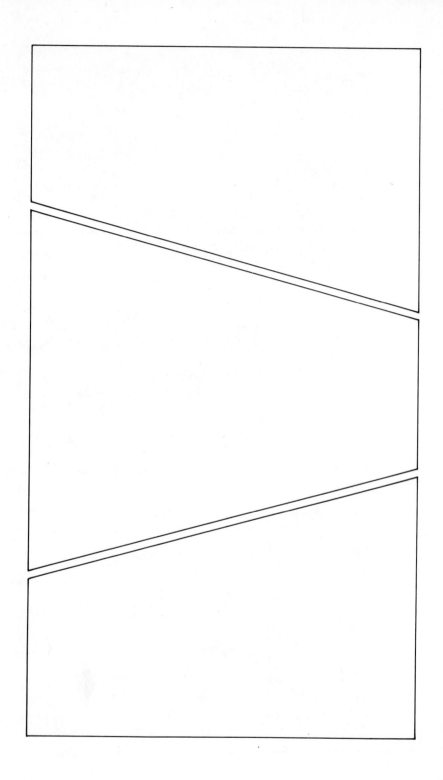

Most audiences are gracious to a meeting leader, particularly if the leader appears to be prepared, enthusiastic, and sensitive to the audience. Seasoned meeting leaders also know that each audience usually has one or more of these:

- Continuous talker
- Fighter
- "I know more than you"
- Quiet one
- Withdrawer

- Sidetalker
- "Takeover leader"

Since each of these problem participants can be recognized, we have provided *Cues* and *Tips for Coping* with them.

• THE CONTINUOUS TALKER

Cues

Asks to comment briefly and then talks for fifteen minutes

Answers every question before others have a chance to comment

Invariably says nothing while speaking

Tips for Coping

When asking for comments, look at the opposite side of the room from where the continuous talker is sitting.

Interject a summary when the continuous talker appears to have no conclusion in mind.

Ask the continuous talker to record the ideas of others and serve as secretary and minutes keeper.

• THE FIGHTER

Cues

Looks angry even before you have begun to speak

Vetoes all suggestions

Uses the phrase, "It won't work"

Tips for Coping

Remember that the anger the fighter feels has, in most cases, nothing to do with you directly. The anger may be because:

You remind this person of someone else

You represent the organization the individual serves, and he or she is angry with the organization

You have kept this person from accomplishing something which he or she may have put off for five or six months and would not be doing now anyway, but in the back of the person's mind, thinks he or she might have

Smile frequently at the fighter and, if possible, mention one of his or her recent accomplishments.

Confront the fighter directly. Acknowledge the attitude by saying, for example: "Paul, you look like you are very upset. Have I said something that particularly bothers you?" Or, "Paul, I've noticed you are angry. Can I help?"

• THE "I KNOW MORE THAN YOU" EXPERT

Cues

Cites additional references for every observation you make, such as:

"*The Insurance Journal for New Zealand* covers your point in significant detail."

Asks questions to see if you are familiar with obscure references

Asks a question, then proceeds to answer it before you've had a chance to comment

Tips for Coping

Tell the participants there will be ample time to discuss your comments during the last twenty minutes of the meeting.

Tell the person you are completely ignorant of the references, the experts he or she cited, and appreciate the information. Provided that you are an expert, the rest of the audience will see how tedious the "I know more than you" expert is.

- ## THE QUIET ONE

Cues

Blushes when his or her name or department is mentioned

Takes abundant notes

Is ill at ease throughout the meeting

Tips on Coping

Gently ask the quiet one to comment on an issue when you know that he or she has the information. After the quiet one has commented, comment on how helpful this information is to the success of the meeting.

Ask the quiet one to record key ideas on the flipchart. This should relax this person because then he or she knows that there is a reason to be at this meeting.

Sometimes it's best to leave the quiet participant alone. On occasion, people prefer to use a meeting as an opportunity to reflect and observe. This right should be protected provided that this does not influence or negatively affect the rest of the group.

- ## THE WITHDRAWER

Cues

Avoids eye contact; will frequently look around the room or at a light fixture, the wall, the floor, or the curtains on the window

Pushes away from the meeting table or takes a seat in the back of the room when everyone else is sitting up front

Doodles and sketches pictures on a note pad during the meeting

Tips for Coping

Regardless of the efforts made to avoid looking at you, continue to try to establish eye contact with the person. Although this may seem, at times, to require nearly standing on your head, this is better than trying to avoid him or her.

Ask the withdrawer to take meeting notes; encourage involvement.

● THE SIDETALKER

Cues

Chats with the person sitting next to him or her

Sends messages in folded-note fashion to others at the meeting

Makes comments and quips under his or her breath

Tips for Coping

Stand near or behind the individual when talking, thus reducing the opportunity to chat with a neighbor.

Stop talking when the sidetalker chats with a neighbor or sends a message across the room.

Tell the sidetalker that you didn't hear his or her comment and ask the person to repeat it.

● THE TAKEOVER LEADER

Cues

Attempts to take control of the meeting by standing up and writing on the flipchart or blackboard

Brings up an item for discussion that is not on the planned agenda

Disagrees frequently and loudly with the leader on how the meeting is being handled

Tips for Coping

Never sarcastically offer this person the chance to run the meeting because he or she will gladly take you up on it.

Do not allow yourself to get involved in a debate with the takeover leader. Instead, ask the group to comment on every suggestion he or she makes.

DIFFICULT AUDIENCE
CHECKLIST

	YES	NO
• Do I know how to handle the continuous talker?		
• Do I know how to handle the fighter?		
• Do I know how to handle the expert?		
• Do I know how to handle the quiet one?		
• Do I know how to handle the withdrawer?		
• Do I know how to handle the sidetalker?		
• Do I know how to handle the takeover leader?		

SUMMARY

This chapter discussed techniques for coping with problem participants. It has been our experience that regardless of how fantastic an audience is, a meeting leader should be aware that there is always someone in every group who poses a very real threat to the success of a meeting. The tips provided here should help you deal with this reality.

Handling a difficult audience requires patience and preparation. To make sure that you're ready, complete this checklist. If you answer "no" to any question, review this chapter.

PREPARE
FOR DIFFICULT
QUESTIONS

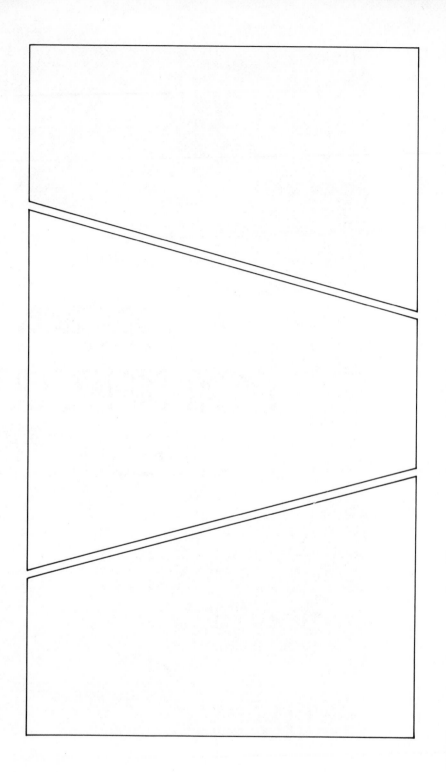

Can you answer difficult questions?

To many, even experienced meeting leaders, the most difficult part of a meeting is the question-and-answer period. Why? Because you have been in control up to this point. Let's face it—now you're a sitting duck. The participants can ask any questions they want and you must answer them.

Here's what happened to a friend of ours. She was a college professor teaching business and finance for the first time. In one of her first lectures she reviewed the structure of contemporary banking in the United States. At the end of her two and a half hour discourse, a student raised his hand and asked: "Where does the World Bank fit into this scheme?" Despite the fact that she knew what the World Bank was, she knew she couldn't explain exactly how it fit into the banking structure without doing some research. However, without hesitation, she gave the first answer that came to her. The students listened attentively and didn't seem to realize that she didn't know what she was talking about, or they were kind enough not to tell her. After the class, she made a vow . . . Never again! From now on, she would admit when she didn't know an answer, find it, and tell the students in the following class. She never again wanted to experience that awful fear of being found out. Handling answers to questions is touchy, tricky, and often troublesome because the person answering:

- Feels "put on the spot"

- Becomes defensive

- Finds it hard to keep an entire group interested in the answer to the question of one person

- Believes that answering "not-anticipated questions," if the answer is inaccurate, may later prove embarrassing

TIPS FOR HANDLING QUESTIONS

These tips will ensure that a question-and-answer period proceeds smoothly.

PLAN EITHER A SPECIFIC TIME FRAME TO HANDLE QUESTIONS AND ANSWERS OR INTERMITTENT QUESTION-AND-ANSWER SESSIONS HELD TO A NARROW TIME FRAME.

Since questions can often get a meeting completely off track, it is wise to schedule a particular time or times to handle them. This technique also allows the leader to get the meeting back on track or conclude the meeting without appearing awkward.

Prevent the awkward silence once the question-and-answer session begins by saying: "I've allowed twenty minutes for handling questions. I'm sure my remarks caused some of you to have some questions. Now, I'll be glad to answer them."

A second technique is to ask the group a particular question about your remarks. For example, you could say: "Did I make myself clear on the point about the decline of international trade? Do you agree with my observations?"

A third technique is to ask an acquaintance to ask the first question, since a first question often gets a discussion going.

REPEAT EACH QUESTION ASKED.

This rule is basic. Why do you repeat a question before you answer it? It allows you to:

1. Assure that everyone in the room hears the question

2. Be sure that you are responding to the correct question

2. Have the time to think of the answer you want to give

WHEN RESPONDING, MAINTAIN EYE CONTACT WITH ALL AUDIENCE MEMBERS.

Many meeting leaders make the mistake of having a dialogue with the individual who asks a question. This eliminates involvement with the rest of the group.

During the question-and-answer period, answer the question asked by keeping eye contact with everyone in the room. As you near the end of your answer, look again at the person who asked the question. Check to see that you get an indication that you have answered the question satisfactorily.

WATCH OUT FOR "AUNT MILLIES."

An "Aunt Millie" question is: "My Aunt Millie tried your suggestions and as a result she broke her gift shop's photocopying machine and it cannot be repaired."

If the leader responds to this question, "That couldn't possibly be," he is defaming the "Aunt Millie" of that audience. If he answers, "Are you serious? Oh, how terrible," he is defaming his own idea. The only successful way an individual can respond to an "Aunt Millie" is by repeating the question through a generalization and responding in a generalization. For instance, the speaker could respond, "All the people who have followed my advice have not had similar results. Or if they have, they haven't told me about it. I would like to know the particulars of what occurred. Perhaps, after the meeting, you could tell me the details."

THANK THE PERSON WHO HAS ASKED A QUESTION.

Make the audience member feel positive for having asked a question. As we all know, it takes courage to ask a question in a room filled with people. So reward these individuals. Statements such as "Good," or "Great," or "I'm glad you asked that question" not only reward the person who asked the question, but also makes the leader appear to be totally in control.

NOD YOUR HEAD WHILE LISTENING TO A QUESTION, EVEN WHEN YOU KNOW THE ASSUMPTIONS ON WHICH THE QUESTION IS BASED ARE FALSE.

Often a leader hears a question based on a false assumption. Your first reaction is to interrupt the questioner and correct him or her. A better approach is to let the person ask the question as you nod your head in agreement. Once the individual has finished, after repeating the question, you can correct the individual's erroneous assumption.

KEEP A "I DON'T HAVE ALL THE ANSWERS" NOTE PAD AND PENCIL HANDY FOR NOTING SUCH QUESTIONS.

There will always be questions you cannot answer, regardless of your expertise. Rather than trying to "fake it," simply comment on the value of the question asked and indicate that although you don't know the answer, you will note the question and get the answer for the person. Once you have noted the question, you are under contract to get the answer.

For example, at one particular meeting, a leader was asked to explain why the policy he was advocating was being used despite a law prohibiting its practice. The leader admitted he honestly didn't know. He simply noted the question and said, "I'll check this out and get back to you."

During the coffee break, he called his personnel department and learned that the law was applicable only on a statewide basis, not a federal basis, the area he was discussing. He later presented the questioner with the correct information.

CLOSE THE QUESTION-AND-ANSWER PERIOD ON THE UPBEAT.

For the question-and-answer period to be especially meaningful and memorable to the participants, the leader should close the question-and-answer period by summarizing the answers, commenting on the nature of the questions, and noting what has been of particular interest. The final touch is to thank the participants for the excellent questions they have asked.

In addition to these techniques, a meeting leader must be familiar with the most frequent types of legitimate questions he or she will hear. These are presented below.

TYPES OF QUESTIONS

According to Jack Hilton, a consultant in televsion and corporate communications, you will generally receive five types of questions during a question-and-answer period. Specifically,

- The A or B dilemma
- The irrelevant question
- The absent-party question
- The inconsistency trap
- The hypothetical question

Each of these is easily recognizable and can be handled with advance preparation. Prior to your meeting, ask your staff for a list of questions or topics they think will come up.

A professor of marketing we recently met was asked to meet with a group of chemical industry specialists to discuss marketing research. Prior to the meeting, he asked his associates to prepare a list of possible questions or topics that might come up at the session. Following the meeting he reported that they had accurately predicted the possible questions by approximately 95%. He was prepared for his meeting.

The five types of questions are now reviewed in detail.

THE A OR B DILEMMA

Typically, this question is: "Would you rather have A or B?" In most cases there may be a best answer; if there is, go for that option in your response. On the other hand, the best option may not be A or B; it may be something else. In either case, be prepared to take the initiative.

While meeting with a group of marketing specialists, the following question was presented to a training manager.

"As a training manager, would you rather have a salesperson call you with a packaged solution or first try to identify your needs and expectations?"

Because the training manager had anticipated the question, the manager responded:

"To be successful with me I want a salesperson to just ask me my needs and expectations. I'm open to using packaged programs; however, I want the salesperson to tell me if the programs require modification based on the needs of my environment."

The manager took the initiative to identify what was expected from anyone making a sales call in the training area.

THE IRRELEVANT QUESTION

The irrelevant question has little to do with the topic or subject of the meeting. When responding to this type of question, you may have to ask:

"Do you mean . . .?"

At this point you want to take the response and bridge back to the subject of the meeting.

"Oh, now I understand; well let me put that in perspective . . . ."

At a meeting of financial executives, a banking officer was asked:

"How does your bank handle loans to personal friends?"

Since the purpose of the meeting was to discuss raising interest rates, the question seemed out of place. The manager asked:

"Do you mean, do we have variable loan rates at the bank?"

The response was:

"No, I want to know if your bank officers give special favors to their friends."

This brief exchange allowed the bank manager to decide what he wanted to communicate.

His response was:

"Oh, now I understand; our banking policies outline the loan rates to our customers regardless of the relationship of the parties involved in the transaction."

By asking a question, the manager was able to draw out more information. The manager knew where he wanted to go and what he wanted to communicate.

THE ABSENT-PARTY QUESTION

Generally, this question will be phrased as:

"What do you think John would say?"

Fortunately, this question is easy to handle. The best response is a direct:

"I don't want to guess what John would say. Why don't you ask him when you see him?"

THE INCONSISTENCY TRAP

This type of question is a favorite of reporters dealing with politicians.

The most famous example might be the question asked of George Romney during the 1968 primaries.

"You used to be a hawk, now you're a dove."

Romney's response was:

"I was brainwashed."

His "brainwashing" response not only cost him the primary, it finished him in politics.

The outcome may not be as severe in a business meeting. Don't be reluctant to say "In '78 I felt A, in '80 I feel B."

THE HYPOTHETICAL QUESTION

The hypothetical question is easy to recognize. The question will start with:

- "If . . ."
- "Let's say . . ."
- "Let's suppose . . ."
- "Let's look into the future . . ."

When dealing with this type of question, you have two options: First, you could reject the question—"I'm not a prophet; I'd rather not speculate about the future" or second, you respond with an "Iffy" response—"If what you say is true, I suppose that is possible." You may also consider quoting someone else— "According to Jim, our company economist, interest rates will go up 3% in the next quarter."

In dealing with questions, Hilton suggested the following:

In my experience questions are preceded by a preface. If you remember two points, the question-and-answer period will be easier:

- Listen closely to the question and concentrate on the question. Pick out the major points of the question.

- In your response, address points; don't answer questions. Reject those damaging points you don't want to deal with.

SUMMARY

Remember the key points outlined in this chapter:

- Plan a specific time for a question-and-answer period.

- Prepare for questions before the meeting. Ask others what questions they might anticipate; then find the answers.

- Repeat each question before you answer to ensure that:

Everyone has heard the question

You have understood the question

You have taken time to think through the answer you want to give

- When a participant asks a question, your voice, language, and attitude should indicate that you are glad to answer the question.

- Keep eye contact with everyone in the room when you answer a question so that everyone stays involved.

- If you do not know the answer to a question, say so. Find the answer later.

- Be sure that questions are answered to the questioner's satisfaction.

- Identify the type of question you have been asked and respond appropriately:

The A or B dilemma

The irrelevant question

The absent-party question

The inconsistency trap

The hypothetical question

The following checklist will help prepare you for the question-and-answer portion of your meeting.

DIFFICULT QUESTION CHECKLIST

	YES	NO
• Have I planned a specific time for questions and answers?		
• Did I ask other people to submit questions to me before the meeting?		
• Have I read advance questions and thought through possible answers?		
• Have I practiced responding to possible questions?		
• Do I know the five kinds of questions and how to recognize them?		
• Do I have a particular viewpoint on the subject that I'm prepared to support?		
• Am I prepared to say that I don't know the answer to a question?		

ASSIGN AND DISTRIBUTE FOLLOW-UP WORK

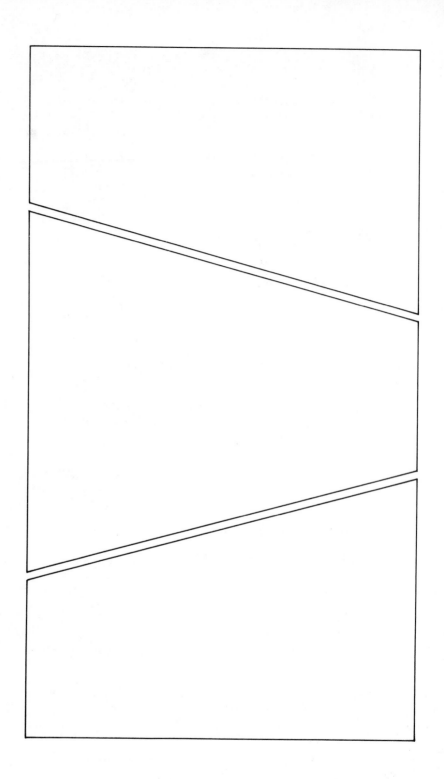

The basic program for all meetings is to make decisions and to formulate action plans.

How do you keep the energy and enthusiasm generated in a meeting so that the work the participants agreed to do is actually accomplished?

This chapter addresses this issue by answering five critical questions most meeting leaders have about delegating work.

1. Who should do the work?

2. How should the work be assigned?

3. When should the work be completed?

4. What should the work look like when it is presented?

5. Should I expect the work to be done as well as if I had done it myself?

Let's briefly review each of these points.

WHO SHOULD DO THE WORK?

As a meeting leader, do you believe in your participants' ability to do the work assigned at your meeting? Well, you're not alone. There are disadvantages to consider when you delegate work. Some of these are:

- The work will not be done correctly.
- It will not be done according to schedule.
- Participants will resent being assigned work.
- Participants won't care about the ultimate impact of the work enough to do a thorough, high-quality job.

However, there are these advantages:

- When work is assigned, others learn how to solve the kind of problem that only the meeting leader could solve previously.
- By assigning the work, there will be increased involvement and interest in committee work.
- The meeting leader is freed from the burden of doing this additional work.
- When work is assigned to several participants, the work is finished faster than when it is assigned to only one individual.

As we review these advantages and disadvantages, it becomes clear that there is a greater value in assigning work to participants. This allows the person in charge of a meeting to carry out the basic principle of management:

TRUE MANAGEMENT IS ACCOMPLISHING RESULTS THROUGH THE COMMITMENT OF OTHER PEOPLE.

Once the decision has been made to assign the work to others, a question must be answered:

HOW SHOULD THE WORK BE ASSIGNED?

The participants should understand the significance of the work they are assigned. Before the meeting ends and the work is delegated to the meeting members, answer these questions to be assured that this is the case. You should be able to answer "yes" to each question.

- Has the scope of the assignment been clearly communicated?

- Has the research required to complete the assignment been fully explained?

- Has the appearance and content of the final document been described?

- Has the presentation of the final document been discussed?

- Have the real and arbitrary time constraints been reviewed?

- Have the time commitments and constraints of those working on the project been reviewed to assure that this additional assignment can be handled?

- Have milestones and final completion dates been mutually agreed upon?

- Will doing the job well—showing thoroughness, problem-solving ability, clear organization, and the ability to explore the problem above and beyond the original assigned scope—be valuable for:

The person's career?

The goals of the department and organization?

- Has it been made clear that successful completion of the assignment will benefit a participant's career in the company?

It is also useful to discuss how and when follow-up meetings will take place.

When assigning work, the meeting leader needs to consider whether the work should be assigned to:

- One person

- A subgroup of two or three people

- A task force of several people

Work best suited for one person is a task of relatively limited time scope and research requirements. If assigned to one person, the individual should know that the work to be completed is part of a career objective rather than a burdensome duty. Meet with the individual, review how the work should be approached, and set up opportunities for review of the assignment before the final project is to be presented. This should eliminate either surprises or disappointments in the final package.

A small subgroup of two or three people is effective if the problem can best be solved by a division of labor. Appoint a head of the subgroup who can provide progress reports. The meeting leader should suggest dates for the subgroup to meet and perhaps provide a suitable location for the meeting.

Task forces are advisable for projects that require a relatively long period of time. For instance, you might want to assign a task force for finding speakers for a year-long professional association education program. The task force can discuss the kinds of speakers the organization should invite and then divide any work to be completed among its members.

WHEN SHOULD THE WORK BE COMPLETED?

Be sure that calendars are brought to meetings to enable you, the meeting leader, and the meeting participants to have an opportunity to commit to deadlines for milestones and actual completion of projects and to note dates to review work in progress.

WHAT SHOULD THE WORK LOOK LIKE WHEN IT IS PRESENTED?

The meeting leader should tell the participants the kind of report that is expected: whether it should be an oral or a written report. Be specific. Describe exactly what you want.

For example:

"The report should include visual aids, charts, graphs, examples, and perhaps pilot test results."

You will be pleased with the final document when you provide the details participants need to complete the assignment correctly.

SHOULD I EXPECT THE WORK TO BE DONE AS WELL AS IF I HAD DONE IT MYSELF?

Every meeting leader can expect and should only accept work done as well as he or she would have done it, as long as these points are followed when assigning the work:

- A meeting was held to help the individual or individuals involved establish a modus operandi for accomplishing the task or tasks at hand.

- The value of the assignment to an individual's career objective has been communicated.

- The assignment has been enthusiastically and positively presented.

- Realistic completion dates have been noted in the meeting leader's and participant's calendars.

SUMMARY

Work assigned at meetings will be completed and completed correctly by meeting participants if:

1. The assignment is thoroughly explained.

2. Attention is given to assigning the work to the appropriately sized group to handle the problem.

3. The final report format has been discussed with those involved.

4. Agreed-upon deadlines are realistic for both the meeting leader and participants.

This checklist will be most useful if reviewed before and after every meeting.

FOLLOW-UP WORK
CHECKLIST

	YES	NO

- Was I prepared to explain the assignments thoroughly?

- Did I consider how large the group should be to handle this problem?

- Did I discuss the report format?

- Did we agree on realistic deadlines?

- Did I remember to ask the participants to bring their calendars?

- Do the assignments fit our company's long-range goals?

- Did we identify who would do the work?

WHEN THE MEETING ENDS

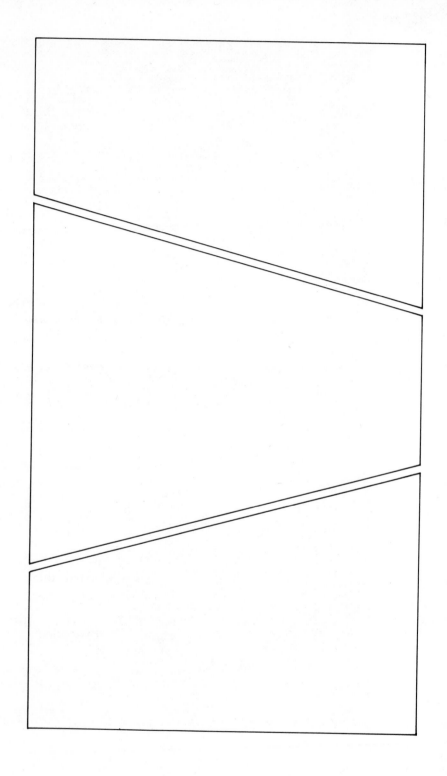

One of the most interesting studies our research for this book uncovered said that people more often remember the way a meeting ends than either the middle or the beginning of the meeting. To make the close of a meeting memorable, meeting participants should:

1. Feel ownership for what has occurred during the meeting.

2. Know that they have an action plan for carrying through the decisions reached at the meeting.

3. Have a positive attitude about what has occurred at the meeting.

Here are several techniques that will help you accomplish these three goals.

MEETING PARTICIPANT OWNERSHIP

"Ownership" means that the meeting participants believe their input has influenced the outcome of the meeting. Moreover, they are ready to accept responsibility for carrying out the decisions.

Participant ownership is achieved when participants *develop realistic solutions* that can be implemented. The purpose of your meeting is action-centered. Participants take action to discover solutions to problems when the meeting leader uses brainstorming, buzz groups, and prework.

BRAINSTORMING

The meeting leader describes a problem, perhaps even noting it on a flipchart or blackboard, then discusses the characteristics of the problem. Then he or she tells the participants that three or four minutes will be devoted to a discussion of this problem only.

Ground rules for the brainstorming session include:

1.   All ideas will be recorded on a flipchart or blackboard.

2.   No idea may be criticized.

3.   As many ideas as possible will be considered during this time period.

This brainstorming technique was developed by Alex Osborne and described at length in his book, *Creativity in Action*. Osborne points out that this technique, when used effectively, can save companies millions of dollars.

For example, brainstorming paid off handsomely for an aluminum company. Here's how it was used. Management called all their production managers into a meeting. Management identified the problem as the inability to compete successfully with another company in the marketplace due to product similarity. The participants were asked to describe any solutions they had to this problem. Each idea was noted on flipcharts arranged around the room. Hundreds of ideas were garnered in a very short time. Among them was one that generated chuckles at the time it was offered: quilted tinfoil.

When top management reviewed the list of suggestions, this particular one stood out. Quilted tinfoil subsequently became a new product idea. It generated a whole new use for tinfoil. It eliminated the need to use broiler pans for cooking turkeys and roasts. That brainstorming session saved the aluminum company.

BUZZ GROUPS

Once a problem has been defined, another technique that generates solutions to problems is to divide meeting participants into buzz groups. Each buzz group discusses the problem, develops a plan for solving the problem, and presents their solutions to the other participants.

PREWORK

Many meeting managers describe a problem in a memorandum distributed to all meeting participants before the meeting. Participants are asked to come to the meeting prepared to discuss *solutions only*. The advantage: Little time is wasted at the meeting reviewing the problem, and maximum time is devoted to discussing solutions.

All these techniques to develop realistic solutions to problems can work successfully. The important point to remember is: A meeting leader must carefully "stage" a procedure for unearthing solutions to problems.

MEETING PARTICIPANTS ACHIEVE OWNERSHIP FOR THE MEETING WHEN THEY HAVE SIGNIFICANT RESPONSIBILITIES FOR CARRYING OUT THE SOLUTIONS TO PROBLEMS.

Meeting participants willingly accept interesting, often demanding assignments that are considered significant undertakings that will challenge their capabilities and stretch their imagination.

OWNERSHIP FOR THE MEETING IS INCREASED IF PARTICIPANTS MUST CROSS-COMMUNICATE AFTER THE MEETING.

Devise reasons for creating channels of cross communication among meeting participants so that they see each other as "comrades-in-arms." When meeting participants feel they belong to a particular group, and identify with that group, meeting ownership increases. "Thanking the participants" adds immeasurable value to their sense of ownership. With a small group, attempt to personalize your thanks to each meeting participant. Thank-you's should describe accomplishments the group has achieved for you—in particular, how they have helped solve a real problem. Allow sufficient time for this thank-you so that it is sincere. Send a letter to each meeting participant, after the meeting, thanking them for their involvement.

A good barometer to use for measuring participant ownership of the meeting you have conducted is to watch for signs of interest. For example, do the participants ask: "When will the next meeting be scheduled?" or "When will we follow up on this meeting?" These questions are sure cues that participants are committed.

Use this checklist to assure that your action plan is in place:

ACTION PLAN CHECKLIST

	YES	NO

- Has an overall solution to the problem been agreed on?

- Have specific milestones for achieving solutions been identified?

- Have meeting participants accepted responsibility for implementing the necessary steps for solutions?

- Have meeting members agreed to specific assignment completion dates?

- Has the action plan been recorded?

- Has the group discussed the previous success of the action plan?

- Has the group determined that the action plan indeed provides solutions?

- Has a backup action plan been considered?

CONCLUDE YOUR MEETING ON A POSITIVE NOTE

At the end of the meeting, the meeting participants should know that something worthwhile has happened and that they contributed to making it happen. Here are several techniques to use to conclude a meeting on a "high note."

1. Conclude the meeting by restating the meeting objective. Briefly describe how this objective was reached.

2. Summarize the meeting events.

3. Conclude the meeting at the scheduled time.

4. Ask each meeting member to give a brief analysis of what he or she believes the meeting accomplished.

Then see that the minutes taken during the meeting are sent to each participant within twenty-four hours after the meeting.

SUMMARY

Remember that the close of the meeting is the part most people remember. For this reason, each meeting leader will want to take this portion of the meeting very seriously. The three most common complaints about meeting closes are:

1. The meeting continues even though it is no longer necessary to continue.

2. No decisions are reached at the meeting.

2. The meeting ends late.

Here are several points to keep in mind:

- Limit the discussion time for each subject.

- Be open to all alternatives.

- Don't feel that you have to cover all the issues at one meeting.

- Postpone unplanned topics until another time.

- Clearly identify follow-up items in a post-meeting memo describing: who is to do what, when, where, how, with whom, and by when.

- Use follow-up phone calls or written follow-up memoranda to see if help is needed for the completion of the project.

- Have a backup plan ready for work that isn't completed correctly or on time.

Ask yourself these questions before your meeting and review them once the meeting has ended. All your answers should be "yes."

MEETING INVOLVEMENT CHECKLIST

	YES	NO

- Will we brainstorm each issue so that every view is considered?

- Will we brainstorm possible solutions to each problem?

- Will we brainstorm possible problems that might result from each suggested solution?

- Will I allow each participant a chance to be heard?

- Will I ask the quiet group members to describe what is on their minds?

- Will I strive for consensus, a decision *everyone* can live with?

- Will I bring a bell to the meeting and ring it every time the participants get off course?

- Will I, if the conference is lengthy, allow adequate time for phone calls, bathroom breaks, recreation, and meals?

ONE-ON-ONE MEETINGS

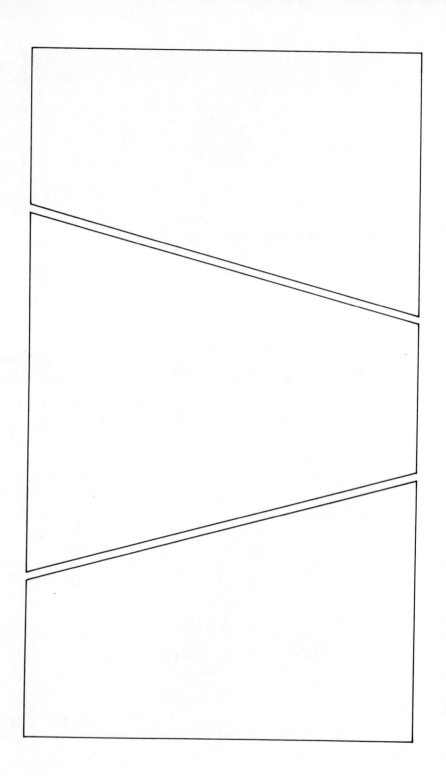

Each day we participate in one-on-one meetings. Often the preparation, conduct, and follow-up to these meetings require the same degree of thought and effort as a meeting with six or two hundred people. Unfortunately, most people neglect to apply the same careful planning to a one-on-one meeting as they do for larger ones. This chapter describes techniques to improve two frequent types of one-on-one meetings.

Our research for this book disclosed that the two most common one-on-one business meetings held are:

1. Meeting with your manager

2. Performance appraisal meetings with a subordinate

An example of an update meeting with a manager is described below.

A certified public accountant had been upset about the way one of his clients had recorded entries in its journals. When he met with his superior to discuss his concern, his manager told him to ignore the errors. During several subsequent update meetings, he insisted that the entries were wrong and that something should be done to correct them. The manager told his subordinate simply to drop the matter. The arguments during these discussions finally became so heated that their relationship disintegrated. Realizing that this was affecting his career and that his manager had become his enemy, the accountant decided to tell his manager he would drop the matter.

However, at a subsequent meeting, before he could say anything, his manager told him he had already contracted an independent auditor to consider the matter. After the review, the decision was made in the subordinate's favor. Now the subordinate was worried sick that he had permanently alienated his manager. Had he, he wondered, "won the battle but lost the war"?

The sequence of meetings eventually damaged the relationship between the subordinate and his manager so badly that the subordinate quit the firm.

The second type of one-on-one meeting discussed in this chapter are performance appraisal meetings. Here, both the manager and subordinate want to assess how well work is being accomplished, identify areas that need improvement, and then build an action plan to correct any problems and needs found during the performance period.

Both of these one-on-one meeting situations require the highest form of listening skills. Rule One for one-on-one meetings is *listen intently.*

KEY IDEA FOR ONE-ON-ONE MEETINGS: LISTEN INTENTLY

To help you identify how often you have one-on-one meetings as described here, take a few minutes to complete the "One-On-One Meetings: Listening Situations Checklist." Then study the following guidelines, which will improve your ability to listen intently.

ONE-ON-ONE MEETINGS: LISTENING SITUATIONS CHECKLIST

ONE-ON-ONE MEETING	PURPOSE OR OBJECTIVE	FREQUENCY OF SITUATION		
		OFTEN	SOMETIMES	NEVER
A. Performance appraisal	• Assess work, areas needing improvement, and provide an action plan.			
Coaching	• Help employee in terms of job duties and responsibilities.			
Counseling	• Work with employee who has off-the-job problems that affect work situations.			
Status report	• Update on status of a project or report			
Advice	• Advice and input on a proposal or conclusion			
Problem solving	• Help in solving a problem or reaching a decision			

GUIDELINES FOR LISTENING INTENTLY IN ONE-ON-ONE MEETINGS

Described below are essential guidelines for your one-on-one meetings. Remember, meeting with your manager or subordinate requires the same, if not more, effort than all other meetings. You must (a) *plan* the meeting, (b) *organize* your discussion agenda, and (c) achieve a known and desired *outcome*.

1.   Prepare Both Yourself and the Other Person in Advance.

Write exactly, point for point, what you want to accomplish (your hoped-for outcome) at the meeting. When you ask these questions, you can determine your approach and the amount of time required for the meeting.

> "What do I want out of this meeting?"

> "Do I want to give my manager information?"

> "Am I asking for input or am I seeking a decision?"

After determining the desired outcome, make sure that you:

- Know the questions you want answered before you go into the meeting
- Can identify a single topic as the primary purpose for the meeting
- Have several alternative topics you are prepared to cover
- Have communicated to the other person, either in writing or orally, a description of the purpose of the meeting and how long you estimate the meeting will take

Here is how you could tell your manager your meeting objective:

> "I believe I'll need twenty minutes of your time tomorrow to cover the new purchase decision."

This indicates both the amount of time you will need and the topic you want to cover. The advantage here is that you avoid surprising your manager.

Another critical issue to consider is when to meet with your manager. You should know the best time. Is your manager a morning person or an afternoon person?

One author's manager prefers to hold meetings before 9 a.m. so that his day is uninterrupted by his staff. The other author's manager prefers holding meetings after 4 p.m. when his phone is quiet. When choosing a time, ask yourself:

"Does my manager need the morning to answer phone calls or to respond to his or her manager?"

If that's the case and there isn't any urgency for the meeting, schedule it in the afternoon. If your manager has a monthly staff meeting or a departmental meeting that requires preparation, don't schedule your meeting for that day.

2. *Organize the Meeting.*

When you present a problem to your manager, be specific. Start the meeting by describing the problem, its causes, and your recommended solutions. You may want to suggest who should oversee the solution, how long the problem should take to solve, and in what department the solution should be handled. Your proactive attitude will help your manager make a decision to act.

A word of caution: Don't go into the meeting with a closed mind. Be prepared to ask your manager to suggest solutions. When you ask your manager for ideas and recommendations, he or she feels involved in the ultimate solution to the problem. The following case history illustrates this point:

An employee met with her manager to discuss the progress she was making contracting a guest speaker for an upcoming conference. The manager asked: "Well, how are you coming with our guest speaker?" The employee responded directly: "I know you asked me to get a particular speaker, Mr. Foster, and quite frankly I can get the speaker at an acceptable honorarium. However, I've done considerable research into the background and experience of this speaker, and I don't believe he is as good as you thought he would be. In fact, my research shows that the speaker probably would not do the kind of job we feel is essential for our company." Without hesitation, the manager said: "Good, I'm glad you found that out. Select a speaker whom you consider appropriate."

The fact is that before this meeting, the employee suffered several weeks of anxiety worrying about telling her manager what she thought he didn't want to hear.

Most people are concerned about what their manager will think of their ideas. This is natural since that raise or promotion may depend on your ability to "tell it like it is."

3.   Discuss One Topic at a Time.

Discussing one topic will avoid the chance that you'll get sidetracked. Present a brief history of the problem—some background on the topic you will cover—in a memo to your manager prior to the meeting. This will also help you clarify your purpose. This way your meeting will be more meaningful for both you and your manager.

During your meeting:

- Explain possible solutions and demonstrate that you've explored the alternatives.

- Summarize your conclusions.

- Ask questions to find out if your insights match your manager's views.

When you present a recommendation, never assume that your manager has the same knowledge base as you have.

For meetings in your manager's office, think of each meeting as a formal presentation. When appropriate, prepare flipcharts or other visual material to enhance your presentation and aid understanding. Small desktop flipcharts and easels are available and are frequently used by sales representatives for presentations to customers. Diagrams or a few key statements on a poster board will help highlight the points you want to make.

4. *Tell Your Manager What You Really Think About a Problem Rather than What You Think He Wants to Hear.*

When involved in this sort of meeting with your manager, use open-ended questions such as: "How do you feel about what I've just said?" or "Could you give me your ideas on how this situation could be improved?" This will encourage your manager to give you the information and feedback you need to do your job.

5. *Be Open to Your Manager's Views.*

Look for signals about how he or she feels about the situation you describe. Seek out your manager's views with such questions as:

"How do you feel about what I've suggested?"

"What do you see as the pluses and minuses of this idea?"

"What is your major concern with what I have just said?"

Once you've asked for your manager's views, be prepared to hear them out. No fair cutting off the person with comments like "Yes, but" or "Well, don't you see. . ." Nod your head and listen.

HOW TO CONDUCT AN "ENLIGHTENED" PERFORMANCE APPRAISAL

The one-on-one meeting held to give a subordinate performance feedback is sufficiently problematic for most managers that it deserves special attention. The remainder of this chapter reviews techniques for handling this all-important meeting.

"Surprise" is the word most frequently heard when a subordinate describes his or her view of a performance appraisal. Common responses during the sessions are:

"I never heard that before."

"I thought I had done a good job."

"Why wasn't I told before this?"

"Why did these comments have to wait until the end of the year?"

In fact, we recall one young man who during his performance appraisal yelled to his manager at the top of his lungs, "Why didn't you tell me?" because the manager said that he had noticed for over a year that the young man never spoke up.

Removing the surprise element can easily be done by applying the following rules:

1.   *Avoid the Once-a-Year Performance Appraisal.*

In many companies, the performance appraisal takes place only once a year. Feedback, documenting problems, and performing the evaluation are left to that "time of the year." When the appraisal does take place, there is insufficient time to provide an effective evaluation.

Feedback should be given on a regular basis. This way there are no surprises during the annual review meeting. Your willingness to commit to the time required contributes to the effectiveness of your appraisals.

Consider how preposterous it would be for a parent to give a child feedback only once a year: similarly for a manager.

2.   *Avoid the Win-Lose Situation.*

A strong performer is easy to evaluate. The meeting requires little time and is frequently an informal, relaxed situation. Both you and your subordinate leave the meeting feeling good about the process. On the other hand, conducting a performance appraisal with an unsatisfactory worker can create a difficult, threatening, and time-consuming experience for both of you. To minimize the negative factors in this type of meeting, develop a "road map" to use during the appraisal. Think of the upcoming appraisal in terms of three phases:

- Preparation

- Discussion

- Follow-up

● **PREPARATION**

Allow sufficient time to prepare for the appraisal session. Let the appraisee know, in advance, the date and the time the appraisal will be held. For example, send a memo and state:

"Your performance appraisal will be held May 24 from 10 a.m. to 12 noon in my office."

In the memorandum, tell the appraisee to come prepared to discuss past performance.

As part of your preparation, review the subordinate's project sheets or reports, which will help you identify specific accomplishments and results since the last review. This documentation is extremely important when evaluating the unsatisfactory performer, since your observations must be specific. Comments such as:

- "Your attitude is bad."

- "You project a negative image."

- "Your communications are poor."

may in fact be true. However, unless you can show how this behavior negatively affects the work the subordinate has been assigned, it is best not to give this type of evaluation. If, however, you find a project the subordinate was assigned but didn't complete, you are then in a position to say:

"The report you were assigned to write about our new product was never completed. As a result, we were unable to sell management on the idea and we did not complete our market penetration as planned. I estimate this unfinished assignment cost the company $200,000 in potential profits this past year."

Identify in writing the strengths and weaknesses of the appraisee. Usually, one or two phrases are sufficient. Focus on performance—on what the individual does. Maintain the appraisee's self-esteem but be prepared to show the effect a specific weakness had on work performance.

THINK DEVELOPMENT!

When you do this, you know it will take time to correct any weaknesses. However, it's better to overcome one or two problems at a time than to overwhelm the appraisee with a laundry list of weaknesses.

How you identify strengths or weaknesses depends on known standards or objectives previously agreed to. Any weakness should be accompanied by a suggestion for correction. Establish a "preliminary" action plan and timetable for improvement, even though the final action plan will not be developed until you hold the appraisal meeting. And, like any other meeting, be prepared to present an alternative.

Finally, write down the outline or précis of your subordinate's performance and be prepared to give the subordinate a copy of it during the discussion. This activity will force you to review all items—minimizing the chance you will back away from a distasteful job.

DISCUSSION

The morning of the performance appraisal, clear your calendar. Before the appraisee arrives, inform your secretary that you don't want to be interrupted. Set a specific time for the appraisal, for example, two hours. Remember to review the "Listening Situations Checklist" on page 151 because you are now ready for the discussion phase of the appraisal process.

Welcome the appraisee to your office, shut the door, offer coffee, be friendly, and spend a few minutes in idle chatter. Select a topic such as a hobby the appraisee may have in order to establish a relaxed atmosphere.

Begin the appraisal by reviewing the purpose of appraisal, stressing the importance of career development. Ask the subordinate to identify his or her accomplishments. For instance:

"Joan, you will remember that when we scheduled this meeting, I asked you to prepare a list of your accomplishments and a brief summary of your performance. Let's go over these first."

As you listen to the description, you may wish to modify your plan or thoughts. Unless you have given this person day-to-day feedback, your views could come as a surprise and the situation might lead to conflict.

Be prepared to deal with any anger or resentment. Strive to be direct and specific. If you detect that the appraisee's views are totally out of sync with yours, concentrate on attitude rather than performance. Finally, it may be necessary for you to say: "I sense that you feel you've done an outstanding job this past year. Frankly, I need your help in determining why our views are so far apart. Here's how I view your record . . . ."

When your views are not that far apart, paraphrase the appraisee's thoughts. Present your view of the performance of the subordinate. Keep your comments work related. Talk in terms of specific skills or weaknesses that affected an agreed-to objective. Focus on why the deterioration has taken place. Don't rush into this. Rather, allow sufficient time to develop your ideas and to state the facts as you see them.

Summarize frequently. "So far, we've talked about . . . now, let's go on to . . . ." Ask the subordinate if he or she has understood what you've said by asking the person to capsulize your comments.

During your preparation for this meeting, you gathered the facts. Sometimes an appraisee will not agree on a specific point during the discussion. You may explain:

"Well, you may not agree with me, but that's the way it is. I can appreciate that hearing criticism may be unpleasant; however, the facts speak for themselves. I've identified, from my files, the following specific examples of unsuccessful performance."

With an employee whose performance can be improved, develop an action plan with the person's assistance so that you have his or her commitment to correct the situation.

DON'T FORCE YOUR PLAN

Appropriate phrases such as:

- "What do you think you can do to improve these areas we've discussed?" or

- "What is the first area you would like to work on?"

should engage the employee in both the appraisal and the improvement process. Then say: "Try it my way for the next few months. Then we'll get together to discuss your progress."

On the other hand, if the situation seems to be getting out of hand, you should say: "Look, we don't seem to be getting anywhere. Why don't we both think about this for a few days. Let's schedule another meeting for Tuesday at 2 o'clock."

Simply because you have scheduled three hours for the appraisal doesn't mean that it must be completed in just that time. Finish the meeting when it is done. End on a positive note. Your objective is to come as close to a win-win situation as possible. Both of you should leave the discussion feeling that the time was valuably spent.

A FEW POST-DISCUSSION NOTES

When you give your impression of performance, have the written summary statement fairly represent your discussion. If this is the employee's first appraisal and you use a numerical rating system, explain the meaning of the numbers as well as the standards used for each numerical level. Ask the subordinate to sign the written evaluation you have completed before you submit it. Give the appraisee a copy to keep.

FOLLOW UP

Agree during the appraisal discussion or shortly thereafter on several follow-up meetings to measure the progress of the action plan. Use these follow-up meetings to gauge performance and attitude and to offer comments and reactions. As a result of these meetings, the following year's performance appraisal should go smoothly.

SUMMARY

Remember, we are asking you to think of one-on-one conversations as "meetings" and not just an everyday occurrence normally performed in your job. We covered the two most common meetings held—meeting with your manager and a performance appraisal meeting. Using the "Listening Situations Checklist" we believe you will also improve these meetings by applying the how to's we have presented in this book.

These techniques are a starting point. They are meant to remind everyone who runs a meeting—from one-on-one to one hundred—that the success of a meeting depends on preparation, content, and the meeting process.

Here's an exercise for you. Before your next performance appraisal, answer these questions. Hold the appraisal meeting only when you can respond "yes" to all these questions.

PERFORMANCE APPRAISAL CHECKLIST

	YES	NO

- Have I reviewed the "Listening Situations Checklist"?

- Have I provided the appraisee with enough time to prepare for our meeting?

- Do I have all the necessary reports, project sheets, and other factual data to conduct the appraisal?

- Can I identify specific work activities that relate to the weaknesses or strengths I have identified?

- Have I observed and recorded performance based on the key requirements for the job?

- Did I recognize outside factors, for example, changing requirements that affect performance?

- Have I set aside enough time to write the appraisal?

- Is the written appraisal geared to the appraisee's needs?

- Is my performance summary consistent with the key points in my appraisal?

- Is the appraisal directed at behavior the person can change?

- Do I have a follow-up plan to go into effect after the appraisal?

AFTER
YOUR MEETING

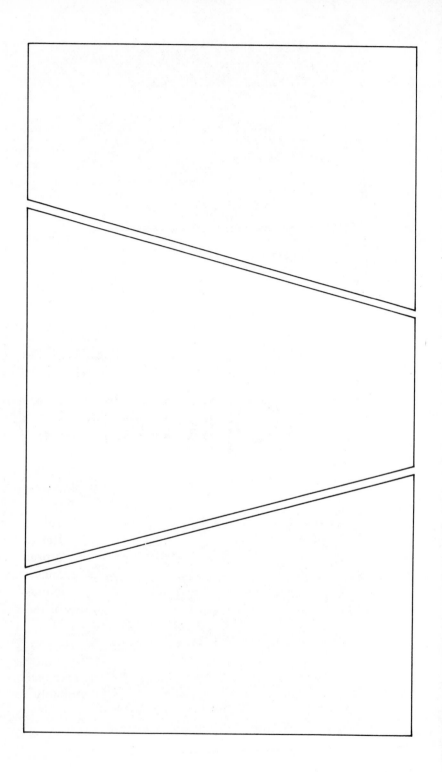

A faculty departmental meeting was held at a major university in 1975 to decide whether or not to allow a pregnant college instructor to continue teaching. There were neither precedents nor university rules to guide the meeting participants with their decision. After two and a half hours of discussion of the implications of a pregnant instructor continuing to teach during her pregnancy, the participants decided that they were in no position to make a decision—and the instructor continued to teach until the day she delivered.

Even a decision not to make a decision is a meeting result. And this example, even though no decision was ever reached—the decisionless outcome of the meeting was probably the most desirable result.

As a meeting leader, what can you do to evaluate your meeting results? In this chapter we provide you with an explanation of such evaluation techniques as:

- Participant evaluation forms
- Informal questionnaire
- Time checklist
- Attitude index
- Results checklist

As you'll see, any one of these techniques used alone or with others will help you focus on the results and value of your meetings.

PARTICIPANT EVALUATION FORMS

The participant evaluation form is effective for both formal and informal meetings. When deciding to use a particular evaluation form, you'll need to ask: What questions should be on the form?

Typically, these forms rate participant reaction to the meeting leader, meeting room, use of time in the meeting, and evaluation of the meeting. An example follows.

MEETING EVALUATION FORM 1

On this Meeting Evaluation Form, questions 1 and 2 use the semantic differential. The semantic differential provides an opportunity for a participant to evaluate a point based on a scaled rating system and it allows those reviewing the form to get an indication of how a person feels about a particular item.

MEETING EVALUATION FORM 1 (Cont.)

_____   _____
Name of Meeting   Date of Meeting

Directions: Please give your candid reaction to this meeting by rating it on the five-point scale shown below. Circle the appropriate number on the scale to represent your evaluation. Your comments are needed to help us continually improve our meetings.

1. What is your overall evaluation of the meeting?

   1 2 3 4 5

   Nothing was   Much was
   accomplished   accomplished

2. Evaluate the meeting in terms of your use of time.

   1 2 3 4 5

   A waste of   Good use of
   my time   my time

Questions 3 and 4 use the open-ended question format. Open-ended questions allow the participant to speak about matters they have on their mind.

3. What would have improved the meeting? Be specific.

4. What should the leader have done? Be specific.

Another, similar form is shown here:

MEETING EVALUATION FORM 2

1. How relevant was this session to my present needs?

_____ (please check)

| Highly relevant | Fairly relevant | Slightly relevant | Not very relevant |

2. How probable do you think it is that you will put into action any ideas from the session?

_____ (please check)

| Highly probable | Quite probable | Slightly probable | Not very probable |

3. What do you think might be an outcome in your own situation (if any)?

4. Please give any feedback comments to the leader(s) of this meeting (e.g., about leadership style design of the meeting, content of session, your feelings, etc.)

_____

MEETING EVALUATION FORM 3

PARTICIPANT EVALUATION

To enable us to better conduct future seminars on current topics, we need your opinion of the one you're presently attending. Please complete this form and submit it to the seminar leader at the end of the session.

MEETING EVALUATION FORM 3 (Cont.)

Name of seminar or topic _____

How would you rate the seminar on its overall value to you? (Check one)

Outstanding _____ Poor _____
Good _____   Other (explain)_____
Average _____

_____

_____

What are the strong points or valuable portions of this seminar? (Be specific)

_____

_____

_____

_____

_____

_____

_____

What are the weak points or areas for improvement in this seminar? (Be specific)

_____

_____

_____

_____

For the benefit of the seminar leader, rate his or her effectiveness in the appropriate boxes below. If there is more than one instruc-

MEETING EVALUATION FORM 3 (Cont.)

PARTICIPANT EVALUATION

tor, place all their names in the blank beside the code letter and use the letter when indicating your rating.

Name of seminar leader _____ Code Letter A

Name of seminar leader _____ Code Letter B

Name of seminar leader _____ Code Letter C

	Outstanding	Good Average	Inadequate
1. Overall ability to help me learn, lead the group, and present materials in an under-standing manner.	☐	☐	☐
2. Demonstration of knowledge of subject matter.	☐	☐	☐

In what ways could the seminar leader(s) improve?

_____

_____

_____

What topics would you like to see as the subjects of future seminars?

_____

_____

_____

_____

Our primary suggestion for developing a participant evaluation form:

KEEP IT SHORT

We all tire quickly when asked to fill out a form three or four pages long.

When putting together an evaluation form, should the form include a space for the individual to sign his or her name? You'll notice that neither the first or the second form included such a space, although the third one does. Many people believe that anonymity increases candor when completing these forms. Others prefer to give people the opportunity to record their names. We are inclined to go with the latter technique since people can always opt not to sign a form.

For the best results using participant evaluation forms, follow these suggestions:

- Don't distribute the evaluation form during the meeting. Participants have an inescapable desire to complete a form as soon as they see it. Consequently, when people are given a meeting evaluation form before the meeting ends, they immediately complete the form rather than paying attention to meeting events. As a result, their opinion of the meeting is meaningless.

- Allow sufficient time for completion of the evaluation form at the end of the meeting. As a general rule, it takes thirty minutes to explain adequately how the evaluation form is to be completed and then for the participant to fill it out. Set the stage for the completion of the form. Tell the participants:

  1. Who will read the evaluation forms
  2. That honest, sincere suggestions are appreciated and used

3. That a summary of the meeting comments will be sent to the meeting participants
4. That the meeting comments will be used to build subsequent meetings

Once you have set the stage for completion of the evaluation forms, do not interrupt the group with additional meeting information. Instead, hold all comments until all evaluation forms have been completed. Provide a place where participants can leave their evaluation forms—on a desk, an empty chair, in a carton, with another participant.

Summarize the evaluations and distribute them to all the participants so that they can see that you thought seriously enough about their comments to include this information in a cover memorandum.

INFORMAL SOLICITATION

Telephone calls, drop-in visitors, coffee clatches, airline trips, even cocktail hours serve as excellent opportunities to find out how participants reacted to your meeting. How should you get their response? Ask these open-ended questions:

- "What did you think of the meeting yesterday?"
- "Do you think anyone felt left out of our meeting yesterday?"
- "Do you think we achieved our objective?"
- "How could I have improved the meeting?"

These questions will enable you to learn how people responded to your meeting.

For example, a manager once asked, "What could have been done to run a better meeting yesterday?" It was suggested:

"Using a flipchart at the meeting to record ideas would have provided more structure and organization."

At his very next meeting he used the flipchart to:

- Describe his agenda
- Record participant reaction
- Describe the action plan reached by the participants and completion dates for individual assignments

Sometimes closed-ended questions will also give you the information you need. These questions might include:

- "Did you believe you were able to express your viewpoint during the meeting?"
- "What prevented you from expressing your views?"
- "Cite an example where we got off the track at the meeting."

The informal solicitation technique is the most frequently used. This technique can be a powerful tool when handled with discretion and sensitivity.

Keep these suggestions in mind when asking for information informally. For example, ask participants while their views are still fresh, before their responses are blurred by time or influenced by other discussions.

Set the stage for collecting the data. Try an opening such as: "I want to improve the way I run my meetings." Then take note only of those ideas that will help you improve the way you run them.

Avoid shutting off communications by responding to comments made with remarks such as: "Yes, but . . . ." or "That's not so." or "You're wrong on that." Be prepared to respond positively to the suggestions you are given.

Thank the participants who give you information so that they know their opinion is valued.

THREE SELF-ADMINISTERED CHECKLISTS

Here are three self-administered tests. When the questions are answered honestly and objectively, they will give you reliable information about how well a meeting was received.

Most meeting experts agree that attitude has a vital impact on the success of a meeting. Give serious attention to how each member of the group feels while problem solving at a meeting.

Use this "Attitude Checklist" to measure the spirit of the meeting participants.

ATTITUDE CHECKLIST

	YES	NO
• Did each person participate?		
• Were participants frequently cut off before finishing their thoughts?		
• Did participants avoid other meeting members by looking at the walls or the ceiling or the floor?		
• Did participants fold their arms to resist information?		
• Did participants begin sentences with "Yes, but . . . .?"		
• Was there tension in the room?		
• Were participants motivated to solve the problem or just to dissect it?		

Use this checklist to review and evaluate how well you used your meeting time.

TIME CHECKLIST

	YES	NO*

- Did I start the meeting at the scheduled time?

- Did I review a posted agenda?

- Did my agenda describe time frames?

- Did I manage to keep to the planned agenda time frames?

- Did I cut off nonproductive conversation?

- Did I assign the role of timekeeper to a meeting member?

- Was I flexible about time when necessary?

- Did I end the meeting on time?

- Did I assign the responsibility of taking minutes at the meeting?

- Did I assign dates to follow-up work?

- Did I make sure we allowed sufficient time for:

- An effective introduction?

- An effective summary?

- An evaluation of the meeting when appropriate?

*If you answered "no" to any of these questions, you have an area for improvement at your next meeting.

Without question, the most important question a meeting leader asks is: "Were my objectives achieved at this meeting?" This checklist helps provide the answers and will help to evaluate your overall approach to the meeting.

RESULTS CHECKLIST

	YES	NO

- Did each meeting participant understand the meeting objective?

- At the end of the meeting, did each meeting participant feel that he or she "owned" the problem?

DID YOU

- Have a clear purpose for holding your meeting?

- Know your audience?

- Give sufficient notice to those who were to attend the meeting and explain why it was important for them to be there?

- Prepare an agenda?

- Know the room where the meeting would be held?

- Start the meeting on time?

- Follow your agenda?

- Have minutes taken at the meeting?

- Allow the participants to say what was on their minds?

- Allow sufficient time to discuss complex issues?

*If you answered "no" to any of these questions, you have an area for improvement at your next meeting.

RESULTS CHECKLIST (Cont.)

DID YOU	YES	NO

- Make decisions a consensus?
- Have a question-and-answer period?
- Devise a plan to implement and follow through on decisions reached during the meeting?
- Assign a clear responsibility to each participant?
- Follow up?

SUMMARY

Using an evaluation form may be too formal in your organization. If that's true, try a more informal approach. Keep in mind that the key to improving your future meeting is feedback. By completing the self-administered test honestly and objectively you can also improve your meetings.

Without feedback you may be repeating the same mistakes again and again. Make a commitment that you will evaluate future meetings.

GETTING
YOUR FEET
WET

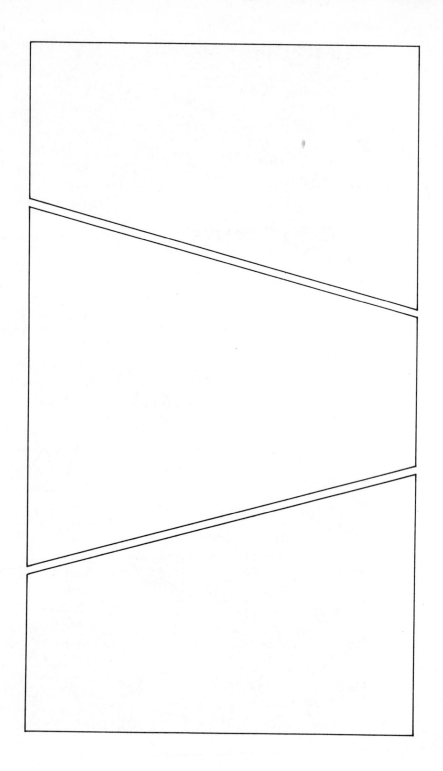

As you prepare for your next meeting, we wish we could be "a fly on the wall" to observe you trying the many possible applications and adaptations of the checklists, ideas, and tools that we have shared with you. As Vince Lombardi said: "Practice does not make perfect. Perfect practice makes perfect." The ideas presented in this book do not automatically convert themselves into successful practice. You'll have to try out and develop the specific skills necessary to run an effective meeting. We believe that through personal adaptation you can pick and choose specific parts of this book that will fit your own unique situation and personal style.

As you "get your feet wet" by diving in and using the material in this book, keep in mind that meetings are here to stay. The effective manager knows that making the best possible use of them will justify diverting personnel from the front lines to the meeting table.

Using this book requires a leader who is willing to risk being creative, imaginative, and effective, a leader who invites and challenges group members to take the same risks. This type of meeting leader will satisfy the needs and expectations of the group.

Start your next meeting as a confident, prepared leader.

Start your meeting on time.

Good luck!

BIBLIOGRAPHY

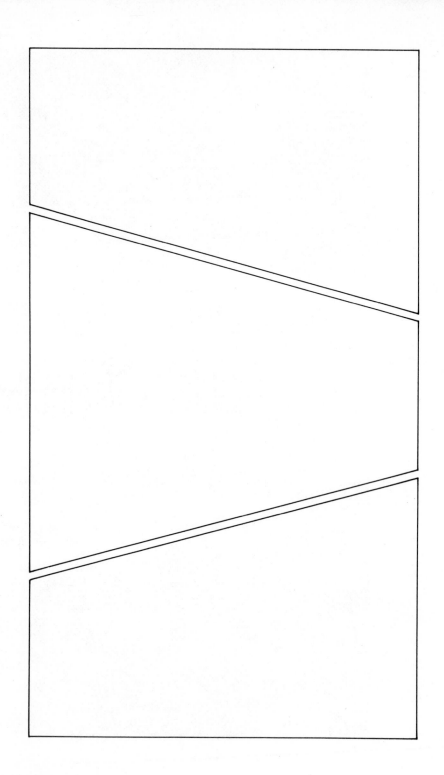

AUGER, B. Y. *How to Run Better Business Meetings.* St. Paul, Minn.: Minnesota Mining and Manufacturing Company, 1972.

BRADFORD, L. P. *Making Meetings Work: A Guide for Leaders and Group Members.* La Jolla, Calif.: University Associates, 1976.

BURKE, W. W., and BECKHARD, R. *Conference Planning* (2nd ed.). La Jolla, Calif.: University Associates, 1976.

BUSINESS EDUCATION DIVISION, DUN & BRADSTREET, INC. "How to Conduct a Meeting." (Dun & Bradstreet Business Series 9.) New York: T.Y. Crowell, 1970.

DOYLE, M., and STRAUS, D. *The New Interaction Method: How to Make Meetings Work.* Chicago: Playboy Press, 1976.

GORDON, W. J. J. *Synectics.* New York: Harper & Row, 1961.

JANIS, I. *Victims of Groupthink.* Boston: Houghton Mifflin, 1972.

JAY, A. "How to Run a Meeting." *Harvard Business Review,* March–April, 1976.

KEPNER, C. H., and TREGOE, B. B. *The Rational Manager.* New York: McGraw-Hill, 1965.

"MANUAL FOR SMALL MEETINGS: Techniques to Make Small Meetings Produce Results." Philadelphia: Brill Communications, 1975.

McPHERSON, J. H. *The People, the Problems, and the Problem Solving Method.* Midland, The Pendall Company, 1967.

MILES, M. *Learning to Work in Groups.* New York: Teachers College Press, 1969.

MILLER, E. C. (Ed.). *Conference Leadership.* New York: American Management Association, 1972.

PARNES, C. J. *Creative Behavior Guidebook.* New York: Charles Scribner's Sons, 1967.

PATTON, B. R., and GRIFFIN, K. *Problem Solving Group Interaction.* New York: Harper & Row, 1973.

PFEIFFER, J. W., and JONES, J. E. (Eds.). *The Annual Handbook for Group Facilitators* (1972–1980). La Jolla, Calif.: University Associates, 1972–1980.

PHILLIPS, G. M. *Communication and the Small Group.* Indianapolis, Ind.: Bobbs-Merrill, 1966.

PRINCE, G. M. "Creative Meetings Through Power Sharing." *Harvard Business Review,* July–August, 1972.

PRINCE, G. M. "How to Be a Better Meeting Chairman." *Harvard Business Review,* January–February, 1969.

PRINCE, G. M. *The Practice of Creativity.* New York: Collier Books, 1972.

RAUSCH, E. "Here's How to Design Your Meeting Message." *Successful Meetings,* January 1976.

RAUSCH, E. "Meeting Can Break the Learning Barrier." *Successful Meetings,* January 1975.

SCHINDLER-RAINMAN, E., and LIPPITT, R. *Taking Your Meetings Out of the Doldrums.* Columbus, Ohio: Association of Professional Directors, 1975.

SCHINDLER-RAINMAN, E., and LIPPITT, R. *The Volunteer Community: Creative Use of Human Resources* (2nd ed.). La Jolla, Calif.: University Associates, 1975.

SIGBAND, N. "Do You Listen When You Hear?" *Nation's Business,* June 1969.

STEINER, I. D. *Group Processes and Productivity.* New York: Academic Press, 1972.

STRAUSS, B, and STRAUSS, F. *New Ways to Better Meetings.* New York: Viking Press, 1951.

THIS, L. "A Manager's Guide to Successful Meetings." *Training and Development Journal,* October 1978.

THIS, L. *The Small Meeting Planner.* Houston, Tex.: Gulf, 1972.